THE ATHLETE'S COOKBOOK

THE ATHLETE'S COOKBOOK

A NUTRITIONAL PROGRAM TO FUEL THE BODY FOR PEAK PERFORMANCE AND RAPID RECOVERY

COREY IRWIN & BRETT STEWART

Ulysses Press

Published by
Ulysses Press
P.O. Box 3440
Berkeley, CA 94703
www.ulyssespress.com

ISBN: 978-1-61243-230-4
Library of Congress Catalog Number 2013938279

Printed in the United States by United Graphics Inc.

10 9 8 7 6 5 4 3 2 1

Acquisitions editor: Keith Riegert
Editor: Lauren Harrison
Proofreader: Elyce Berrigan-Dunlop
Cover design: Double R Design
Cover artwork: athletes © Valeriy Lebedev/shutterstock.com; pancakes © Robyn Mackenzie/
    shutterstock.com; soup © ER_09/shutterstock.com; shrimp © HLPhoto/shutterstock.com;
    mussels © marco mayer/shutterstock.com; burger © Brent Hofacker/shutterstock.com;
    channa masala © Igor Dutina/shutterstock.com
Interior design: Jake Flaherty
Layout: Lindsay Tamura
Interior photographs: page 1 runners © Sogno Lucido/shutterstock.com; page 9 quinoa
    © Portokalis/shutterstock.com; page 37 chili © Charles Brutlag/sshutterstock.com
Index: Sayre Van Young

Distributed by Publishers Group West

To my family—my mother, father, and sister—
who inspire me and exemplify the virtues of healthy living.
And to Erik, my not-so-silent partner,
who holds down the fort while I'm busy creating.
This book wouldn't have been possible without your encouragement and support!

—Corey

Contents

Foreword

When meeting an elite or professional athlete for the first time, one is usually awestruck by their level of performance and athleticism. Shooting the breeze with an NFL Hall of Fame running back at a casual business lunch in Manhattan; meeting one of the NBA's all-time best three-point shooters as he saunters through your office; or even chatting in the locker room with one of your favorite NFL quarterbacks—these are the types of encounters that you can talk about at backyard barbecues or while tailgating at sporting events for years to come. There's no denying that a brush with greatness is a relatively transformative experience for anyone who loves sports.

Once you've been lucky enough, as I have, to chat at length with Steve Young about his legacy and the impact Jerry Rice had on young receivers, or find out what really motivates legendary running back Curtis Martin, you realize that each elite athlete—regardless of the sport—has at least two common threads that tie them all together: sports conditioning and nutrition for performance. One of the first things I asked Herschel Walker was about how he fuels for his legendary 1000-plus sit-ups, push-ups, and pull-ups every day, and each time I've gotten to chat with Dean "Ultramarathon Man" Karnazes during a run, I've asked him how he maintains his caloric intake during epic 300-plus-mile runs or 75 days straight averaging 40 miles as he ran from Disneyland in California to Manhattan, New York City. I want to know what drives these great athletes to be the best they can possibly be mentally, physically, and nutritionally. I literally want to learn what fuels them to achieve their goals and maintain their physiques despite the immense physical toll their chosen sports put on their bodies.

On some occasions I've gotten to spend days at a time living with professional athletes, where I'm able to observe their eating habits, go along for a trip to the grocery store as they shop for their pre- and post-race, and ask questions—lots and lots of questions. Whether they're an international World Champion ITU triathlete, the champion of *American Ninja Warrior*, or a sub-8:30 Ironman athlete (who also happens to be my coauthor on *7 Weeks to a Triathlon*), I'll relentlessly ask them if they ever did this or tried that and why they make the nutritional choices that they do. Some folks are happy with an autograph and a handshake; me, I'd rather know why they chose rolled oats over granola before a time trial or why a bag of Skittles is their post-workout meal on days they're lifting heavy. Bananas? I want to know why and when. Coconut water versus sports drink? I need to know how they made that choice. I may not walk away from the experience with a signed photo that I can hang in my office, but I feel I get so much more out of these encounters. Heck, I've even been able to help diagnose some fueling issues with a couple of these athletes along the way! The next time Paul Amey is tearing up a bike course in a triathlon, there's a good chance I know what he had for breakfast, and he very well may be using a couple of the tips I gave him for keeping his high-watt energy at its peak while he's in the saddle for nearly four hours.

I'm extremely humbled to get to work with such amazing athletes, trainers, and nutritionists, and you'll learn in "How Did We Get Here?" on page 2 how I'm one of the last people on earth who should be so lucky to be in my position. I've never been an elite athlete or chef and have only really been blessed to be a fitness advocate for about a decade. I'm just an average guy who found a passion for getting fit, being healthy, and learning from spectacular individuals in many different areas—and this book is no exception.

Throughout the writing of some of my previous works, I was extremely fortunate to seek out some of the brightest and most talented professionals I could find in their respective fields. In *Paleo Fitness*, I tabbed a world-renowned Paleo expert in Darryl Edwards to take me on a journey into the lifestyle, fitness, and nutrition of his PRIMALity workshops. Throughout *The Vegan Athlete*, I was constantly challenged by Ben Greene to be much more conscious about what I eat and how my nutritional choices affect the world around me. One constant between both of those projects was Corey Irwin, a chef, trainer, running coach, and fitness guru who helped to complete each of those books with her recipes, meal plans, and sound nutritional advice. *The Athlete's Cookbook* gave me the opportunity to take another journey into nutrition with Corey and run the gamut of fueling for elite sports and fitness.

I know you'll find this book to be an amazing resource for new healthy recipes and meal plans to fuel your body and mind to achieve your best!

—Brett Stewart

PART I
GETTING STARTED

Introduction

Eating for athletic performance. It's a major component of an athlete's training regimen. But it's not just about what or how much you eat, it's about when and why you eat it too. To be at your best, you need to eat and exercise in strategic ways that match your goals. That's why this book addresses the "big three" that athletes tend to focus on the most: body fat loss, endurance, and getting ripped.

Of course, the process of becoming an adept athlete isn't just about obtaining knowledge. It's also about strategy and application. What most athletes really want to know is this: "How do I apply the principles I've just learned to my daily life and training?" In short, we athletes need to digest and analyze the knowledge we've obtained, but in the end, we're mostly focused on taking action.

Sports and general nutrition knowledge are useless unless applied, and most athletes are searching for guidance in this area. However, they don't want a biochemistry tome; they want a straightforward, easy-to-follow plan to help them plug in all of that knowledge—to show them what, when, and how to eat for top athletic performance—and ideally, one that's accompanied by a host of healthy recipes to help them escape the boredom of the same food options over and over.

Our primary aim is to address the essential foods that we believe will benefit you the most in terms of athletic performance, nutritional value, and overall health. After all, we athletes put a lot of time and effort into our training by keeping up with the latest sports research and techniques, so why shouldn't we do the same when it comes to the food that we eat?

How Did We Get Here?

COREY: I've been a runner and athlete almost all my life. In school, I played sports like soccer, basketball, swimming, and tennis, took ballet and gymnastics, hit the weights, hiked, skated, and skied. I've done other sports as well, but running has always been my first love. The love affair began early, at age five, when I went for my first run with my dad. Not long after, I ran my first road race, a five-miler, and was completely hooked. I ran track and field in high school, kept running throughout college and into my twenties and thirties, and not surprisingly, am still running today.

Like any other runner, I've had my share of "bumps," stops, and starts, with lots of trial and error along the way. Largely, thanks to my parents, I was raised exercising and eating and cooking healthy food from an early age, but it wasn't until much later that I began to connect the dots between what and when I was eating and the profound impact it would have upon my athletic performance.

I wanted to reap the full benefits of food to take my athletic performance to the next level. So, even though I already had a pretty good handle on nutrition basics, I began paying much more attention to the sports nutrition side and changed my cooking and recipe-writing focus to match. And it paid off big time. I started improving, ultimately becoming even stronger and fitter than I'd ever been before. In fact, in my late thirties, I actually beat some of the PRs I'd set in my twenties, largely thanks to this renewed focus. Sure, I was eating healthy in my twenties, but I wasn't eating strategically. Then, after leaving the traditional workplace for good, I went to work for myself full-time. I became a running coach and realized my athletes needed plenty of support and guidance to help them wrap their heads around proper sports nutrition. More importantly, they needed a go-to reference to make it easy to find delicious, healthy options to maintain peak performance. Thus, *The Athlete's Cookbook* was born!

BRETT: I'm the little fat kid who can't do a single pull-up in gym class and is perennially last-picked for sports at recess.

I'm a 50-pound overweight divorcé in my late twenties working long hours at a job I hate, smoking two packs of cigarettes a day, and getting winded just walking up a flight of stairs.

I'm a 20-plus time marathoner, Ironman finisher, fitness author, model, trainer, and I'm married to the woman of my dreams.

How did I make it happen? I took one step toward a healthy, happy lifestyle. Then, I took another. What was hard at first became easier and easier; the more I stuck with it, the better the results were. Even before the weight melted off, my daily fatigue was gone and replaced by an entirely new drive and sense of purpose. I knew I had a long way to go to be fit, but if I stuck with it, I would never find myself in this "state of blah" ever again. A new healthy lifestyle based around sound nutrition and physical activity transformed my life over the last 15 years—but not overnight. Never in my wildest dreams did I ever imagine this little fat kid knocking out dozens of pull-ups or completing a 50-mile ultramarathon. If I can do it, you can too.

It all starts with just one step in the right direction, and this book is dedicated to help make it as easy as possible. Sure, it will require effort and willpower, but we promise that the longer you stick with it, the easier it will become. Make the investment in yourself to follow the nutrition programs in this book for as little as two weeks, and you'll see positive results that will keep you on track to meet your goals.

About the Book

What matters most is not just what foods can do for you performance-wise over various periods of time, but also what they do to your body in the long-term, which is just as important. This book is written with *both* long-range health and athletic performance in mind, and not just sports performance solely as a means unto itself. Both goals really do go together for total wellness. Not all carbs, proteins, and fats are created equal, nor do they have the same effect upon athletic performance or your health. The point of this book is to provide you with a program that works on BOTH levels. Our nutritional plan is a balanced and healthy program focused on whole nutrient-rich foods that are low in animal-based saturated fats but still satisfying to the taste buds without resorting to refined sugar or processed ingredients.

An underlying philosophical tenet of this book is "everything in moderation." This applies doubly if you're making significant changes to your fitness and eating behaviors. Take it slow and incorporate changes bit by bit rather than all at once. Brett and I are both big believers in making gradual changes that become part of a lifestyle; in order to develop life-long habits, you need to take a long-term view of health and fitness. All sustainable changes start out with small steps that take a few weeks to become a reliable routine. Stick with it and before you know it, you'll have completely transformed your approach to nutrition and fitness, as well as your training, fueling, and physique!

Is there one particular "perfect" way of eating that's right for everyone? Of course not! Every nutrition lifestyle has its merits and deficiencies, and every individual must choose which approach fits them best. It's a personal choice and each athlete is a completely different animal.

As someone who's written recipes and meal plans for various fitness and nutritional lifestyle and fitness books—*The Vegan Athlete*, *Paleo Fitness*, and *7 Weeks to 10 Pounds of Muscle*—I'm well accustomed to dealing with these conflicting viewpoints. For example, *7 Weeks to 10 Pounds of Muscle* advocates lean dairy and meat consumption. However, many vegans cite evidence that these foods are bad for your body (they contain harmful purines, are highly acidic, and upset the body's pH, etc.) and in this camp, there are those who believe that dairy weakens our bones. There's evidence to support these ideas, but there are also those who believe that the benefits of eating dairy and/or meat outweigh the potential drawbacks. In *The Vegan Athlete*, the text shows evidence that the human body wasn't designed to properly digest meat, and yet in *Paleo Fitness*, meat is advocated as an essential part of the human diet. To read each of these books is to take an individual journey through the lens of very specific nutritional goals and requirements. And, even though this book contains recipes of all kinds that are sure to fit into various dietary approaches, our nutritional plan is directed toward a general audience.

How to Use This Book

Eat. Train. Sleep. Rinse. Repeat ... right? If only it were so simple, but real life is far more complicated for each and every one of us!

Even the pro athletes we have worked with can't stick to such a simple routine of fitness, nutrition, and rest, because they're individuals that need to perform a myriad of tasks to function in society and have a life. For the average athlete who has another full-time job aside from fueling, training, and recovery, not to mention a million other day-to-day tasks, it can become nearly impossible to stick to a healthy routine. This book is dedicated to bringing some variety to your nutrition while also helping to pick up healthy habits and fitness routines that can last a lifetime. If you're too busy for a long run or spin class, then spend ten minutes with a jump rope. When travel gets in the way of your normal gym time, then perform some bodyweight exercises in your hotel room. Most importantly, when you're shopping in the grocery store and can't stand to pick up the same foods you buy time after time for the same meals you eat day after day, this book provides over a hundred delicious, nutritious ideas that will help keep your taste buds from dying of boredom.

The recipes and meal plans were specifically chosen to go together with the general workout plans to meet fitness goals, but you're completely welcome to pick and choose to suit your preferences. If you put this book down and only take one thing away from it, let it be this: Too much of a good thing is always a bad thing. Even the healthiest recipes become unhealthy at inflated portion sizes. Every workout program has the ability to make you stronger or break you down if you go too hard for too long and don't rest properly. Remember, everything in moderation!

Frequently Asked Questions

Q. I'm trying to lose weight. I see that many of the foods in this book aren't necessarily low-fat, low-carb, or low-calorie. Won't that make it hard to shed the pounds?

A. Nope. First of all, not all of the foods or recipes listed in this book are intended for body fat loss. Some are geared toward those who have achieved their body fat goals and whose primary interest is maintaining, and/or fine tuning aspects of their body composition (for example, sustaining a consistent body fat percentage, maintaining or increasing their lean muscle mass, etc.) or improving muscle recovery, endurance, and/or their overall fitness.

This book contains three different programs targeted to three distinct goals: endurance, strength, and body fat loss. Each program contains accompanying meal plans, recipes, exercises, and sports nutrition tips that were specifically designed to help you achieve these targeted goals. So if your goal is to shed body fat, then you'll want to follow the body fat loss program.

To this end, keep in mind that consuming fat alone won't make you gain body fat. Our body needs a certain amount of body fat to store energy, provide insulation, make hormones, build cell membranes, facilitate vitamin absorption, and protect our vital organs. If you don't consume enough fat on a daily basis, not only will you probably notice your skin becoming incredibly dry, but your body will literally go into "survival mode" and actually hold onto the very fat you're trying to lose. A better approach is to set your daily intake to 25 to 30 percent fat and shed the pounds by sticking to healthy fats and doing specific types of cardio and strength training exercises that, together, will help you burn fat.

This is why the oils used in the recipes are all healthy fats, and the proteins are lean proteins, including the meat and seafood selections. Plus, the majority of the recipes contain fruits and/or vegetables, even if they aren't vegetarian dishes. Also, many, if not most, of the dishes intentionally contain a diverse array of superfoods.

Q. Why do you call your "weight loss" program a "body fat loss" program instead? What's the difference and why does it matter?

A. There are a few reasons, but let's address the obvious one. A person's body weight is not just composed of fat. The body also contains water, bones, ligaments, tendons, muscle, organs, and other tissues. So when we weigh ourselves on the scale, the reading is really including all of these elements. In fact, if a person were to lose muscle, bone mass, and/or water, they could lose weight without losing any fat.

So, to be more accurate, we've replaced the words "weight loss" with "body fat loss" to describe the goal of this particular program, because that's what most people are really trying to lose when they say "weight loss." Just as you can be out-of-shape with an unhealthy body fat percentage, you can also be fit with an unhealthy body fat percentage, or healthy or out-of-shape with a healthy body fat percentage. You can also be perfectly fit with a higher-than-recommended BMI (body mass index). This is why we recommend that you use body fat metrics, as well as hip-to-waist ratio, to get a better sense of the overall picture—for both health and fitness. Body fat and hip-to-waist ratio are also good predictors of health risk factors.

Q. I'm following a particular dietary lifestyle for health/medical, philosophical, and/or religious reasons (this includes vegan, vegetarian, Paleo, kosher/halal, diabetic, or gluten-free). Can I adapt your programs to meet my needs?

A. Yes, to some degree. Although this book was written for a general audience rather than those following a restrictive dietary program, it provides enough recipes that can be easily modified (via ingredient substitutions or omissions) to suit particular dietary lifestyles. If you're looking for books geared specifically toward vegan or Paleo fitness and nutrition, we suggest that you check out two books that would specifically address your dietary needs, namely *The Vegan Athlete* and *Paleo Fitness*.

Q. I see that your book is filled with a lot of international recipes. This is very different from many other sports-oriented cookbooks. Why did you decide to do that?

A. There are already enough sports-oriented cookbooks out there that primarily focus on classic, continental American cuisine, so there was no need to create another one. Traditional American cuisine is great, and there's nothing wrong with it, but the definition of American cuisine in the modern era has expanded. We're no longer a nation that subsists on dishes like Ambrosia Salad, Chicken Kiev, and Baked Alaska.

I believe that chefs and the cookbooks they write need to stay plugged in to the reality of modern life and also adapt to the everchanging culinary landscape. And that landscape has changed significantly over the past 15 to 20 years. Thanks to advancements in farming, food delivery, and distribution, as well as exposure via the Internet, an evergrowing assortment of international restaurants, an increased variety of online, restaurant, and grocery store food offerings, and much more diverse populations, we now have access to foods that were once unavailable to us ten or fifteen years ago. Foods that were considered to be hard-to-find, "exotic delicacies" have now become much more common. Not only that, but there are now so many different cooking shows and food-related online resources as well. As a result, Americans now eat and appreciate a much wider variety of foods. This cookbook is a reflection of all of these factors, and celebrates America's culinary evolution.

In general, I think these changes are a good thing. Access and exposure to new foods and cuisines not only expands our horizons but also creates new and exciting culinary possibilities for us to try and enjoy. Plus, it's fun to be adventurous.

PART II
THE NUTRITIONAL PROGRAMS

Eating for Athletic Performance

Wanna know a secret? Whether your goal is to get lean, build muscle, or increase endurance, eating right is 80 percent of the battle. Sure, that other 20 percent, exercise, is certainly an important piece of the puzzle, but an athlete relies upon food and drink as both fuel and building materials for a fit, strong body. We are literally what we eat—the amino acids in various protein sources are the building blocks of muscle, carbs replenish necessary muscle glycogen and also aid in muscle recovery and growth, essential fatty acids give us energy for future use, while various other nutrients fortify the body and keep it healthy so we can perform at our best.

Get this part down pat, and the rest of your nutritional roadmap is just a matter of streamlining or tweaking your plans and methods here and there to make additional improvements or changes to complement new goals or to refresh our menus to keep them interesting and our motivation going strong.

"Top 10 Foods" for Athletes

The foods from this section can be mixed and matched to suit individual athletic performance goals. To make this process easier, all of the foods on these lists correspond to matching recipes that in turn plug in to one or more of the goal-oriented meal plans beginning on page 32.

Top 10 Nutritious Carbohydrates

1. VEGETABLES: They're a great source of fiber, antioxidants, vitamins, and minerals, and are one of the healthiest forms of carbs. Several phytonutrients in vegetables fight cancer and disease, and can also help stabilize blood sugar. Leafy greens, cruciferous vegetables (such as broccoli, cauliflower, bok choy, watercress, and cabbage) and allium family vegetables (like onions, garlic, and scallions) are some particularly nutritious selections.

2. **BANANAS:** Rich in potassium, an essential electrolyte, one large banana provides roughly 31 grams of carbs. For both of these reasons, a banana makes a great pre- or post-workout snack.

3. **BERRIES:** Berries like raspberries, strawberries, blueberries, and blackberries are rich in both carbs and antioxidants.

4. **LEGUMES:** These high-satiety foods are an excellent source of carbs. Some healthy options include garbanzo beans, black beans, lentils, and peanuts.

5. **WHOLE GRAINS:** Whole grains like barley, oats, bulgur, wheatberries, and black rice contain soluble fiber that regulates blood cholesterol levels. Whole grains are good sources of resistant starch, which means they take longer to be broken down by the body. So, in other words, they have staying power.

6. **QUINOA:** Gluten-free and high fiber, quinoa also helps regulate blood sugar levels.

7. **WINTER SQUASH:** Winter squash like butternut squash, acorn squash, pumpkin, and spaghetti squash are rich in fiber, vitamins, minerals, and of course, carbs.

8. **SWEET POTATOES:** Carb-rich sweet potatoes are a high-satiety food and are also a rich source of the antioxidant beta-carotene and potassium, an electrolyte essential to athletic performance and recovery.

9. **DAIRY PRODUCTS:** Certain dairy products like milk and yogurt are rich sources of carbohydrates. Due to their high Glycemic Index, it's best to save these foods for post-exercise consumption.

10. **TOMATOES:** Particularly in a concentrated form like tomato sauce, tomatoes are a good source of carbs. Plus they're packed with antioxidants (like lycopene) that can lower the risk of certain diseases, including diabetes, heart disease, osteoporosis, and prostate cancer in men.

Top 10 Lean Proteins

1. **SEEDS AND NUTS:** In whole form or as a spread, nuts and seeds are excellent sources of protein. Stick to raw or dry-roasted seeds and nuts rather than the kind that are treated or cooked in oil. Some kinds like walnuts, flaxseed, and chia seeds are also omega-3–rich as well.

2. **LEAN POULTRY:** Skinless turkey and chicken breast are some of the healthiest, high-protein selections. Poultry contains the highest amount of valine, one of the three BCAAs essential to muscle building.

3. **WILD-CAUGHT FISH:** Not all fish are created equal, nutritionally speaking. Tuna and salmon are among the leanest, highest-protein selections at 35 to 39 grams and 23 grams, respectively, per cup. In particular, albacore and wild salmon are some of the

best choices. Avoid farmed Atlantic salmon, which contains contaminants and also a lower amount of omega-3s and other nutrients. Other good wild-caught fish include haddock, halibut, sole, cod, tilapia, trout, catfish, sardines, and anchovies. Fresh is preferable, but frozen is the next best choice.

4. **LEAN SHELLFISH:** Shrimp, scallops, and mussels are among the healthiest choices.

5. **WHEY PROTEIN ISOLATE POWDER:** Some mixtures are 90 percent protein, but concentration can vary by brand, so be sure to read the labels.

6. **LEAN RED MEAT:** Best choices include buffalo meat and grass-fed beef cuts like eye of the round roast, top round roast, lean ground beef, and top sirloin steak, sirloin tip side steak, and top round steak.

7. **LEAN DAIRY:** Some of the best high-protein dairy selections include hard cheeses, particularly Parmesan, Romano, and Asiago, which are not only high in protein but also low in fat. Of all of the hard cheeses, shredded Parmesan is the highest in protein (38.5 grams of protein per cup), closely followed by Pecorino Romano and Asiago, both at 32 grams of protein per cup. Other great options include cottage cheese, ricotta, mozzarella, skim milk, and Greek yogurt. Many dairy products contain omega-3s as well as leucine and isoleucine, two key BCAAs that help build muscle. Dairy also contains casein and whey, which is a very powerful combination: The former slows down protein breakdown in the body while the latter accelerates protein synthesis, two essential activities for building and maintaining muscle.

8. **SOY:** This high-protein food is available in multiple forms, including edamame, tofu, soy nuts, and miso paste. Protein content can vary depending upon form and variety. Typically, when it comes to tofu, the firmer the tofu, the higher the protein content.

POWER TIP: MUSSELS

Eating mussels can help you to pump up your energy levels and elevate your mood. In fact, they have been known to have natural antidepressant properties. Here's why: The vitamin B12 they contain plays an important role in the body's metabolism. In particular, it helps facilitate chemical reactions (via molecules called cofactors, which are most commonly enzymes), which in turn contribute to energy production, as well as fatty acid synthesis and DNA synthesis and regulation. More specifically, B12 vitamins are involved in many methylation reactions in the body. For example, B12 plays a vital role in DNA methylation, an essential biochemical process that regulates gene expression patterning in cells (i.e., expressing or suppressing genes) and plays a vital part in the normal development of higher organisms. Notably, DNA methylation is involved in the suppression of viral gene expression and in the development of almost all types of cancer. B12 is also essential to the proper functioning of the brain and nervous system. It helps repair damaged nerves and contributes to the manufacturing of important neurotransmitters like serotonin and dopamine. Serotonin regulates mood, appetite, and sleep patterns, while dopamine regulates movement and how we experience pleasure. So, now you might be able to see why the B12 in mussels might contribute toward making you feel good.

9. **LEGUMES:** Black beans, kidney beans, chickpeas, lentils, and peanuts are some of the healthiest selections.

10. **QUINOA:** Quinoa is technically a seed, although it's sometimes misclassified as a grain. It's a decent source of protein at 8 grams of protein per cup.

Top 10 Healthy Fats

1. **EXTRA-VIRGIN COCONUT OIL:** Coconut oil is predominately composed of saturated fat (92 percent). However, unlike most animal-based saturated fats, this plant-based saturated fat can't be readily stored in the body, so it's burned as energy instead.

2. **HAZELNUT OIL:** This oil is high in cholesterol-fighting monounsaturated fat (82 percent).

3. **FLAXSEED OIL:** Rich in omega-3s, believe it or not, flaxseed oil contains more omega-3s than fish oil does.

4. **WALNUT OIL:** Walnut is another good source of omega-3s. It's composed mostly of polyunsaturated fats.

5. **FISH OIL:** Known for its high omega-3 content, this oil can be found in many different types of fish, including salmon, albacore tuna, and sardines, to name just a few.

6. **ALMOND OIL:** This oil is high in omega-6s and monounsaturated fat.

7. **AVOCADO OIL:** Avocado oil has a high monounsaturated fat content, which can reduce LDL cholesterol (i.e., the "bad" kind of cholesterol), and also reduce the risk of heart disease and bone fractures. It may also lessen UV-induced cellular damage, which is good news for outdoor exercisers. It has the highest smoke point of any plant-based oil, so it's ideal for high-heat cooking.

8. **EXTRA-VIRGIN OLIVE OIL:** This oil consists of mostly monounsaturated fat (78 percent) and it's minimally processed, so it retains most of its antioxidants, including vitamin E and oleocanthal, an anti-inflammatory substance that works similarly to ibuprofen and may also help prevent joint pain and exercised-induced asthma. So try incorporating some olive oil in your diet, as it may reduce reliance on nonsteroidal anti-inflammatory drugs like ibuprofen. Olive oil has a short shelf life, so store it in a cool, dark place.

9. **SESAME OIL:** Comprising equal parts mono- and polyunsaturated fats, sesame oil may improve blood sugar stabilization and blood pressure levels, which is due to its high lignan content, which acts as an antioxidant.

10. **SUNFLOWER OIL:** A neutral, light-tasting oil, sunflower oil is high in monounsaturated fats. Go with the high-oleic version for the best health benefits.

OTHER HEALTHY CHOICES: Safflower oil, expeller-pressed canola oil, hemp oil, grapeseed oil.

Top 10 Fat-Burning Foods

1. **COCONUT OIL:** Yes, believe it or not, this is a fat that actually helps to burn, well, fat. Not only that, it also provides an immediately usable, sustainable source of energy, which makes it the perfect choice for athletes. So how can the saturated fat in coconut oil be such an effective fat-burning mechanism? The answer lies in its chemical composition, or more specifically, its atomic structure: Coconut oil contains lauric acid, a medium-chain triglyceride (MCT). Unlike the long-chain triglycerides found in other types of fats, MCTs have a shorter chain of carbon atoms, and therefore can be more rapidly broken down by the body and converted into energy. Since the body can't readily store MCTs, it must burn them, thus resulting in an increase in fat oxidation (fat burning) and energy expenditure. And when coconut oil is ingested in moderation, that can lead to weight loss.

2. **HOT CHILE PEPPERS:** Recent scientific studies such as those published in the *British Journal of Nutrition*, the *Journal of Biological Chemistry*, and the *American Journal of Clinical Nutrition*, have shown that the capsaicin, the chemical responsible for hot chile peppers' piquancy, can help speed up your resting metabolism and fat oxidation rates. Capsaicin generates heat in the body through a process known as thermogenesis, in which cells convert available energy in the body into heat.

3. **WHOLE GRAINS:** It takes a lot more time and energy for your body to digest whole grains than processed grains. This is because the tough outer layer (the cereal germ, endosperm, and bran) of whole grains remains intact, and so the body requires more calories to break them down. Contrast this with processed grains, which are stripped of these layers, and it's clear why they are more quickly digested. Whole grains stay

---

POWER TIP: VITAMIN A

At 23,017 mcg per cup, sweet potatoes are extremely high in the phytonutrient beta-carotene, a carotenoid that can easily be converted into vitamin A, which has several important benefits to athletes. That's a higher amount than most leafy green vegetables! Even better, as little as 3 to 5 grams of fat has been shown to considerably improve the body's absorption of both beta-carotene and vitamin A.

So how does vitamin A help athletes? It supports muscle tissue growth by helping to create essential proteins in the body. Vitamin A also helps boost testosterone, which plays a key role in increasing muscle mass and bone density. Vitamin A also has another athletic benefit: It helps oxygenate your blood by supporting red blood cell formation and transporting iron to your red blood cells. And if you want to improve your VO2 max, you'll want to take full advantage of this benefit.

---

in your system longer during the digestion process and thus keep you full for a longer period of time. Good examples of fat-burning whole grains include quinoa, oats (particularly steel-cut oats), and buckwheat.

4. **LEAN MEATS:** The protein found in lean meat requires a lot of energy in order for your body to digest it, even more energy than it takes to burn carbs. Meat has a high thermogenic effect and burns about 30 percent of the calories contained in meat itself during the digestion process.

5. **LEAN DAIRY FOODS:** Some good examples of effective fat-burning dairy foods include low-fat yogurt and eggs. The vitamin B12 in eggs has the ability to break down fat cells. As mentioned above, the body requires more time and energy to digest protein, so protein not only satisfies you by keeping you full for a longer period of time, but also helps to burn fat.

6. **APPLES:** Apples are an abundant source of pectin, which, when ingested, binds to water molecules and restricts how much fat your cells can absorb. Not only that, but the antioxidants they contain may prevent metabolic syndrome, which is characterized by extra weight gain around the waist and is often a prediabetic indicator. Their high fiber content also makes them a high-satiety food. Apples also are rich in the flavonoid quercetin, an antioxidant with some major exercise recovery benefits. For one, quercetin has anti-inflammatory properties. It can reduce exercise-induced oxidative stress, and thus promote post-exercise tissue repair and muscle building. Not only that, but it also promotes joint and cardiovascular health and supports the immune system to boot.

7. **LEAFY GREENS:** Their powerful antioxidants fight cell-damaging free radicals and their bountiful amino acids help improve muscle recovery and growth. Since they're packed with fiber, they'll fill you up and help keep the cravings at bay. After all, a stomach filled with leafy greens is less likely to have room for other less healthy things.

8. **LEGUMES:** Legumes, particularly lentils, chickpeas, black beans, and peanuts, are not only high-satiety, which can help keep off the pounds, but also help regulate blood sugar, which is yet another effective control mechanism to keep cravings in check.

9. **OMEGA-3–RICH SEAFOOD:** Shellfish like mussels and oysters, or oily fish like wild salmon, arctic char, sardines, sablefish, anchovies, albacore tuna, halibut, and mackerel aren't just good for getting rid of post-exercise inflammation. They can also help burn fat by dissolving fat-soluble toxins in the body that contribute to body fat gain. Omega-3s activate enzymes responsible for fat oxidation, and when you combine that with exercise, which increases your oxygen intake, you can burn even more fat. Just make

sure you choose wild-caught over farm-raised varieties because they're significantly higher in omega-3s and much lower in harmful environmental toxins.

10. **CINNAMON**: This warm spice has been shown to help regulate blood sugar levels while metabolizing glucose in the body, thus preventing it from being converted into fat. This not only provides energy but also helps to reduce food cravings, both factors in maintaining a healthy body composition.

OTHER HEALTHY CHOICES: Pine nuts, oats, eggs, green tea, olives, bananas, citrus fruits, asparagus, watermelon, sweet potatoes, garlic (and other allium family vegetables like onions).

The Eating Protocols

Outlined here are the eating protocols, which have been specifically designed to help you achieve your athletic performance goals. Think of each protocol as a roadmap with its own unique set of nutritional principles and guidelines that form the foundation upon which all other elements of each program, including the meal plans and recipes, are based.

FIRST THINGS FIRST: Pick the set of eating protocols that best suits your primary goal—body fat loss, endurance, or strength. Then follow the corresponding meal plan for that program. It's as simple as that.

Please be aware that each protocol differs significantly from the others in its methodology, food combinations, and food timing strategies. So, to produce the best and most efficient results, start by following only one set of protocols and stay the course until you achieve your objectives. Consistent, continual application is key to your success, so this is why you should avoid mixing and matching protocols or switching midstream. You can always change to another protocol after you achieve your initial goal.

FOOD TIMING: For each of the three eating protocols, food timing is a key structural component: The order in which the body burns carbs, protein, and fat has a direct bearing upon the order in which they should all be consumed. The closer you adhere to the food timing guidelines, the more effective you'll be in achieving the goals of the nutritional programs in this book.

THE BIGGER PICTURE: The eating protocols incorporate whole, unprocessed foods that best fit each athletic performance goal according to their nutritional properties. They are based upon biochemistry, long-term health-focused strategies, and common-sense eating behaviors. To be clear, they are *not* centered around the consumption of low-calorie, low-carb, or low-fat foods, particularly if they aren't naturally occurring in this state. Most foods that claim to have these "low" attributes have been altered by manufacturers to be this way, and so they contain harmful chemicals and processed ingredients that will end up doing your body more harm than good for all their advertised so-called benefits.

Taking shortcuts to drop a few pounds isn't really worth it if shortens your lifespan in the process. For people who've been operating in this headspace for a while, it can take some time for the blinders to come off. However, once we start viewing our food as part of the total preventative health package instead of as a temporary Band-Aid or short-term "weight-loss aid" that operates in its own separate orbit (often to the exclusion of all else, including our own health!), that's when we truly begin to break out of our bubbles and connect the dots between our day-to-day habits and our long-term health prospects. The light bulb goes off once we realize that many of our neatly compartmentalized health-related thoughts and behaviors are no longer serving us as well as we once thought. But that's actually a really good thing, because the larger takeaway is this: Now that our eyes are open, we're ready to put these newly acquired insights and knowledge into practice. And it doesn't matter what stage of life we're in; it's never too late to make changes for the better. Once we can see that our actions and intentions are no longer closely aligned, it's time to change the roadmap. What can be learned can be unlearned, and we replace it with new and more effective knowledge to put in its place. By following these eating protocols, you'll actually be achieving two goals: In the process of improving your athletic performance, you'll also be remapping a more effective pathway to better health.

How to Make Your Food Work for You

FOOD AS FUEL: The human body gets its energy and cellular "building materials" from three basic forms of fuel: carbs, protein, and fats. Your body is pretty efficient about the way it goes about its business of converting this fuel into energy (via metabolic chemistry). It doesn't like doing any more work than necessary, so it goes for the most readily available sources of energy first—carbs.

Due to their chemical structure, carbs can be quickly broken down into simple sugars (glucose). Since they're most easily converted into energy, carbs are burned first. When there aren't any carbs left to use for energy, your body will turn to fat next. It takes a bit more energy to burn fat (9 calories per gram, to be exact) but it's certainly much easier to convert into energy than protein. The body will rarely resort to using protein as a primary fuel source, except under extreme circumstances (like starvation). Of course, this is something we actually want to prevent, since an athlete wants to use protein to build muscle, not to break it down for energy. Protein is composed of amino acids, which the body can break down and then reconstitute into new proteins, which are then used for protein synthesis, among other functions.

So, the bottom line is this: If you eat carbs first, that's what your body's going to burn first. This is fine if you're not trying to lose body fat and are primarily concerned with endurance. (Endurance athletes need to eat both carbs and protein *before* their workouts, or else they're going to seriously bonk on the trail.) However, if you want to lose body fat or build muscle, you need to wait until *after* your workouts to consume carbs. And here's why: You'll need those carbs for glycogen replenishment to aid in muscle recovery, repair, and growth.

When you eat carbs, your blood sugar spikes. The higher the Glycemic Load (GL) of a particular food, the higher the spike. As a result, insulin will kick in to regulate blood sugar and will increase blood flow in order to do this. This, in turn, has an anabolic net effect, accelerating protein synthesis and as well as glucose and amino acid uptake to muscle cells, as well as other cells in the body. It also facilitates glycogenesis (the conversion of glucose to glycogen) for storage in liver and muscle cells, which is essential for muscle repair and growth. Insulin also has anticatabolic effects as well: It protects your muscles by preventing the protein they need for growth from being broken down and converted into fuel. And that means bigger muscles for you.

But that's not the only reason carb timing is so essential to improving health and athletic performance: While you're sleeping, your body gets to the point where it's used up all of its glycogen from the carbs you ate earlier in the day. Of course, your body is no longer receiving carbs or any other type of food for that matter (unless you just so happen to sleepwalk and then stumble into the kitchen for a bite to eat). As there's no longer a need to regulate carbs in the bloodstream, your insulin level drops. Once all of the glycogen's used up from the carbs you ate earlier in the day, the body turns to stored fat as its primary energy source in order to maintain itself, and thus transitions from glycogen-burning to fat-burning mode.

We can also maximize our energy as well as our fat-burning and muscle-building abilities by using foods, activities, and various situations to our advantage. It's already well known that our bodies heat up when we exercise. This process is known as thermogenesis, because our bodies are generating heat during that period. This is one of the reasons that our fat-burning rate is particularly high during what's known as the post-exercise "afterburn" period. But did you know that, in addition to exercising, there are specific strategies we can use to burn fat at a higher rate? We also burn fat when we eat certain foods that create a warming effect in the body. This is why some foods like cinnamon and chile peppers are thought to boost metabolism, since the heat they generate helps to burn fat at a higher rate, which in turn, produces energy. Also, in general, since fat requires oxygen to burn (or oxidize), any activities that increase our oxygen capacity, like, say, exercise, which oxygenates the blood, organs, and tissues, also boost our fat-burning capacity as well. Hyperbaric chambers are thought to have the same effect. And while you sleep, you might notice that at some point in the middle of the night, you start to perspire. This is because your body is burning fat while you sleep. Again, this is due to thermogenesis.

In fact, when you wake-up in the morning, your body's still burning fat. Not coincidentally, the morning is also when your body's at its most insulin-sensitive as well. In other words, your insulin is highly responsive at that time. It's at the ready, just hanging around waiting for "instructions" and, depending upon what you eat, will either start storing fat or burning fat or carbs. In particular, your insulin is primed to respond to carbs like a hair trigger, but won't respond in the same way to fat and (pure) protein, because they have little, if any, effect on blood sugar. (The exception is of course, protein from many plant and dairy sources that also contain carbohydrates, but many of these sources, particularly the plant-based ones, ultimately have the net effect of stabilizing or lowering blood sugar, with the exception of milk and other dairy products that are high in lactose.)

You can even extend your fat-burning window for even longer by waiting to eat until *after* you exercise, or by eating only fats and proteins before your workouts. This strategy isn't recommended for endurance athletes (for reasons I'll explain in the endurance protocol section on page 28) but will work well for athletes who are trying to maximize their fat burn and build lean muscle mass. Just make sure that you eat your first meal of the day within 15 to 20 minutes of finishing your workout to maximize fat burn and proper muscle recovery. Breakfast is often touted as the "most important meal of the day," but when you add exercise into the equation, you'll need to shift your breakfast time around some and possibly redefine what you eat for breakfast as well. One strategy is to eat a high-protein snack before your workout and then eat breakfast immediately afterward, or do the exact reverse. Or, you can skip the snack and then go right to a post-workout breakfast. The choice is up to you. Just remember that *when* and *what* you eat for breakfast are equally important.

Eat some carbs first thing after you wake up? Insulin will signal your body to switch from fat-burning into glycogen-burning mode. What, you wanted to eat strategically in order to burn fat instead? Tough luck, you just lost your chance at maximizing your fat burn through food, but all isn't lost: Go out and get some exercise instead. Or try again with a do-over for tomorrow morning's meal. Why? Because your insulin just gave those carbs their marching orders instead. So, it's off to the glycogen-burning factory they go. However, there's one caveat with glycogen-burning mode: This assumes that you're doing enough activity for your body to actually start burning off those carbs and also assumes that you aren't ingesting more carbs than your insulin can deal with at any one time. In an attempt to manage an overdose of carbs, your body's insulin levels will go through the roof. Sure, all that insulin will lower your blood sugar, which would normally sound like a good thing. However, since glycogen storage space is limited in the liver and muscles, whatever carbs can't be stored as glycogen in these locations must now, by default, be stored as fat instead. Not only that, but your insulin will also signal your body to not release any stored body fat as well. And that just makes it harder to lose body fat. However, if you time and regulate your carb consumption, you'll be able to keep both your blood sugar and your body fat percentage in check.

OK, now before you get ready to swear off carbs for the rest of your natural born life, here's the good news: Despite the bad rap carbs have gotten over the past several years, they really aren't evil. In fact, when they're used strategically—at the right times and in the proper amounts—they can actually be very useful if you're trying to build muscle, lose weight, or power yourself through an endurance event. (We'll get into the specifics of that a bit later, below.) And sure, not all carbs are created equal, and foods with a high GL can spike your blood sugar, but the upside is that high-GL foods will trigger insulin to send glycogen and protein to your muscles for quicker and more effective post-exercise recovery. The lesson here is that all-or-nothing, overgeneralized approaches toward carbs just don't paint an accurate picture of their pros and cons. It's much more complicated than that. It's not just a matter of individual foods; you've also got to be mindful of what you eat and when.

PRE-EXERCISE EATING AND HYDRATION: If you do decide to eat before exercise, regardless of the type of workout you do, be sure to both eat *and* hydrate at least two hours before you exercise. This is very important, as forgetting to do either or waiting until the last minute will create several issues that are easily avoided. For one, it doesn't feel that great to have food and drink swishing around in you while you're working out. Your body needs time to process your food and drink so that you can exercise without having to make a pit stop every 5 minutes. This is particularly unnerving when you're in an area where there are no facilities on the premises or they are exceptionally far away when the urge strikes. Also, eating and drinking too close to your workout time will very likely upset your stomach and/or give you cramps or side stitches. Your body needs time for liquids and nutrients to be fully absorbed in order to maximize their use during exercise. And one to one-and-a-half hours just doesn't cut it either. Believe me, I know. Ideally, if you eat a larger meal than usual or just like the security of knowing you'll feel good before you head out for your workout, three hours of digestion time is even better. This might mean you have to get up earlier if you're a morning exerciser, but again, if you're not an endurance athlete, you also have the option to eat after exercise instead.

POST-EXERCISE EATING AND HYDRATION: Just as important as your pre-exercise nutrition regimen is your post-exercise nutrition. Again, it doesn't matter what type of exercise you do, the post-exercise window for sports nutrition recovery is exactly the same across the board: Hydrate and eat within 15 to 20 minutes of finishing your workout to maximize the athletic performance benefits.

Among sports nutritionists, the general consensus is that there's a very specific ratio, 4:1, or 4 grams of carbs to every 1 gram of protein, that you should consume after exercise in order to help you maintain and build muscle, reduce lactic acid, and replenish your glycogen stores. The post-workout recovery drinks in this book all follow this ratio.

So how much of each do you need after a workout? In truth, the exact amounts of protein and carbs will vary depending upon factors like gender, activity type and level, metabolism, and how much muscle you want to maintain or gain, etc. However, for the sake of simplicity, the general recommendation for post-workout protein consumption is usually between 20 and 30 grams of protein. To figure out how many carbs you'll need, simply multiply the amount of protein you require by four. So, if your post-workout protein consumption is 25 grams, that means you'll need to consume 100 grams of carbs after your workout as well.

To take your post-exercise recovery to the next level, you'll want to follow these specific nutritional guidelines as well:

- Eat lean, protein-rich foods with branched chain amino acids (BCAAs) for muscle repair, growth, and protection.
- Be sure to consume water and foods and drinks containing the essential electrolyte potassium, which is particularly important for hydrating muscle and reducing lactic acid.
- Eat foods with omega-3s to reduce post-exercise inflammation. Inflammation is a natural part of exercise recovery and is essential to the healing and muscle tissue repair processes. However, if you're experiencing abnormal amounts of inflammation due to injury, illness, or other factors, you can eat foods with omega-3s to mitigate this condition.
- Eat foods with a high Glycemic Load immediately after exercise (within 15 to 20 minutes) to spike blood sugar, which in turn will signal insulin to transport essential carbs, protein, and nutrients to your muscles, other essential tissues, and organs via the blood stream. Generally, high-GL foods are not recommended *before* you exercise for all of the aforementioned reasons. However, eating them *after* exercise is a whole other story altogether. The quicker you refuel and rehydrate the more effective your recovery will be.

Goals of
the Meal Plans

Below are nutrition strategies and sample eating schedules for each eating protocol to give you a better idea of how to time your meals, or more specifically, what combinations of carbs, proteins, and fats you should eat and when. Please see the corresponding meal plans section on page 32 for specific sample meals that fit these protocols.

It's important to coordinate each eating protocol with a regular hydration schedule as well, so be sure to drink water throughout the day—during meals and snacks, and anytime in between. On workout days, be cognizant of hydration timing as well, allowing for two hours of spacing between your water consumption and any workouts that follow.

Goal I: Body Fat Loss

Eating to Lose Body Fat

The most effective way to lose body fat is to build muscle. Muscle mass requires energy to sustain, so the more muscle you have, the more energy you'll need to fuel those muscles. Ideally, we want this energy to be burned off in the form of body fat. In order to maximize fat burning in the most time-efficient manner, follow the below meal-timing schedule (page 27) and meal plan (page 32) in conjunction with an exercise regimen that incorporates weight-bearing exercises (whether bodyweight exercises or traditional weightlifting) two to three times a week and 15 to 30 minutes of high-intensity interval training (HIIT) one to two days a week. HIIT involves quick bursts of high-intensity exercise alternated with short recovery periods. Due to the intense nature of these activities, they don't have to be done for very long to be effective, which is perfect if you're crunched for time but still want to squeeze in a workout.

10 Easy Things You Can Do Right Now to Lose Body Fat

Incorporate these changes slowly over time.

1. CUT OUT (OR REDUCE CONSUMPTION OF) SODA: Eliminating soda from your diet is an easy, surefire way to drop body fat. It might seem like an insignificant thing to do, but you'd be surprised how much you can lose in a year by doing this. Replace soda with water and herbal teas. The high-fructose corn syrup (HFCS) and caffeine in soda will destabilize your blood sugar level and put it in freefall, which in turn will keep you hungry and craving more HFCS and caffeine. Because of this, it can be hard to get "unstuck," so to break the cycle, eat fiber-rich, high-protein foods and exercise. The former will fill you up and stabilize your blood sugar while the later replaces a "sugar high" with an "exercise high." Both of these tactics will help you wean yourself off these harmful substances.

2. CUT OUT (OR REDUCE CONSUMPTION OF) FRUIT JUICE: Try to stay away from juice that isn't freshly squeezed as it usually contains added fructose and other sugars. Eating fruit in whole form is much better than just drinking juice. You get the fiber and other nutrients that aren't usually part of most commercially sold juice products, and that gives you a full feeling so you don't consume so much of it. Not only can fruit juice rot the teeth, but certain types of juices have more sugar and calories per fluid ounce than soda!

3. REDUCE OR ELIMINATE ALL PROCESSED FOODS: Get rid of products containing refined sugar, trans fats, and corn syrup (especially HFCS). Refined sugar and corn syrup are not only bad for you in terms of nutrition but they are extremely caloric. If you stop eating processed foods, this will take care of almost all forms of corn syrup. These days, food manufacturers seem to add corn syrup to almost everything, even items you might not ordinarily suspect like hot cocoa and bread. In terms of taste and nutrition, fresh, whole foods are best, but if you must resort to manufactured products, read the labels and look for simple whole ingredients like milk, flour, and eggs. The fewer ingredients, the better. If there are a ton of ingredients that you can't pronounce, that's usually a sign that they're all artificial, so do yourself and your health a favor and just put it back on the shelf. Plus, consider this: Fresh, whole foods have a wonderful vibrant taste and aroma, and are extremely satisfying on multiple levels.

4. ESTABLISH A REGULAR SLEEP SCHEDULE AND GET SUFFICIENT SLEEP: Go to bed at a decent hour and get enough sleep. People who have irregular sleep schedules, or sleep too much or too little, tend to be overweight. Your body clock needs to be regulated, so take care of yourself and get the proper amount of sleep. For most people, this means getting a minimum of eight hours.

5. **GO OUT TO EAT LESS OFTEN:** This doesn't mean that you have to completely eliminate eating out. However, if you make your food at home more often instead of going out to eat so much, you can better control what goes into your food, not to mention that you'll also save a lot of money in the process. Most restaurants in the United States tend to serve portion sizes that are way larger than the recommended serving sizes for individuals. When people are out to eat, they often aren't conscious of this.

6. **START READING LABELS:** Sure, reading labels in and of itself is not going to cause you to slim down or become healthier. However, it will help you become a more aware and informed consumer, and also make you conscious of what you're putting into your body, and that's usually the first step toward improved eating behaviors. Knowledge is empowering. A big part of slimming down is simply becoming conscious of what you're doing and eating. It's fairly simple. If something has a zillion ingredients in it, it's usually filled with chemicals and processed ingredients. If something has just a few ingredients, such as milk, eggs, and flour, it's usually a lot healthier for you.

7. **CUT OUT OR REDUCE EMPTY, NUTRIENT-DEFICIENT STARCHES:** Reduce or eliminate bread and refined flour products and replace them with nutrient-dense carbs. Instead of white bread, bagels, crackers, and white flour–based pastas, eat foods like legumes, sweet potatoes, bananas, and cruciferous vegetables. If you're going to eat pasta, try eating whole-grain or omega-3–enriched pasta instead. Again, you don't have to completely eliminate these foods from your diet; just reduce them. If you bake, try replacing unbleached all-purpose flour with alternative whole-grain flours like oat flour or nut-based flours like almond or coconut flour. (Please note that whole wheat flour *isn't* the same thing as whole-grain flour, nor is it as nutritious. The former has the bran and germ removed during processing, which subtracts over half of its original nutritional value, while the latter retains the entire kernel and thus most of its nutritional value.)

8. **EAT BREAKFAST, PREFERABLY IMMEDIATELY AFTER YOUR (MORNING) WORKOUT:** Utilize the 15 minute after-burn window to help you better metabolize your food intake. If you don't have time to make yourself a full breakfast, grab something like a premade hard-boiled egg and a banana while you're walking out the door. A banana will provide minerals and carbs while the egg provides a healthy dose of nutrients and protein. A handful of nuts will also work as well. It's better than nothing. Remember, breakfast doesn't have to be complicated; just make sure you're getting the proper balance of nutrients in the morning to start you off on the right foot for the rest of the day.

9. **PREPARE SNACKS IN ADVANCE TO TAKE WITH YOU TO WORK AND OTHER DAILY ACTIVITIES:** This can be something as easy as cut-up vegetables and store-bought hummus. Having

these will keep you from grabbing things from the junk food machine when you're desperately hungry at 3 p.m.

10. **EAT REGULARLY:** Some health professionals advise eating three square meals a day with three snacks while others recommend eating six small meals a day. Do what works best for you. (If you're particularly busy, the latter strategy can seem a bit daunting, but it's certainly good for blood sugar regulation, which in turn helps control cravings.) The point is to eat regularly and only eat when you're physically hungry. Tune in to your physical hunger cues. You'll be less likely to succumb to less healthy temptations when you're having a moment of weakness.

The Bottom Line

It's as simple as this: If a food or eating behavior doesn't serve you any longer, then eliminate it. This is how a performance-minded athlete thinks about their training, so why should it be any different when it comes to how they think about sports nutrition?

When you're eating for athletic performance and health, suddenly the path to your goals becomes clearer, because all of the other distractions that were once holding you back are now wiped out of the way. To an athlete, food is fuel, eaten in service of a basic but very important goal: maintaining the body. This doesn't mean that you have to completely strip the enjoyment out of eating food. It just means you might have to reframe your outlook a bit in terms of where food fits into your life. Instead of making food the end goal, it now becomes part of the process, to be enjoyed on your journey to better health and athletic performance. And that paradigm shift can be extremely liberating. To an athlete, food and exercise are both subsets of health. And really, when you learn to enjoy the process of becoming healthy and the feelings of accomplishment that go with it, that can actually make both even more pleasurable.

Meal Timing Schedule

In a nutshell, here's how the program works: On non-workout days and for meals preceding workouts, stick to lean, high-protein foods and low-carb selections, preferably in the form of vegetables like cruciferous vegetables and leafy greens. On exercise days, eat high-protein, carb-rich foods after your workouts. Whenever possible, go for nutrient-dense, carb-rich selections like fruit, whole grains, legumes, and squash; root vegetables like sweet potatoes should take precedence over foods of comparatively lesser nutritional value, i.e., "empty starches" like breads and pasta. Low-carb vegetables may be added to any snack or meal. All fat should be consumed in moderation, with total daily fat consumption not to exceed 25 to 30 percent of one's total intake.

MEAL TIMING SCHEDULE

NON-WORKOUT DAY

7 a.m.	Breakfast: lean protein + healthy fat
10 a.m.	Snack: lean protein
12:30 p.m.	Lunch: lean protein + healthy fat
3 p.m.	Snack: lean protein
5:30 p.m.	Dinner: lean protein + healthy fat
7:30 p.m.	Snack: lean protein

WORKOUT DAY

6 a.m.	Workout
7 a.m.	Breakfast or recovery shake: lean protein + carbs
10 a.m.	Snack: protein + carbs
12:30 p.m.	Lunch: protein + carbs
3 p.m.	Snack: protein + carbs
5:30 p.m.	Dinner: protein + carbs
7:30 p.m.	Snack: protein + carbs

WORKOUT DAY (ALTERNATE SCHEDULE):

5 a.m.	Breakfast: lean protein
7 a.m.	Workout
10 a.m.	Recovery snack: protein + carbs
12:30 p.m.	Lunch: protein + carbs
3 p.m.	Snack: protein + carbs
5:30 p.m.	Dinner: protein + carbs
7:30 p.m.	Snack: protein + carbs

Goal II: Endurance

Eating for Endurance

When it comes to endurance sports, you're going to be out there training for a long while, and that's going to require an enormous amount of energy, particularly in the form of carbs. So, quite literally, you'll want to avoid running on empty. In order to meet these energy requirements, it's very important for endurance athletes to fuel and hydrate well in advance of their workouts, not only to ensure healthy digestion but also to allow enough time for their bodies to process the carbs, protein, liquids, and nutrients they've just consumed in order for them to be readily available for use during exercise: Carbs need to be converted into glycogen for storage in your muscles (and liver), protein needs to be reconstituted into usable proteins that can be readily stored in your muscles, and the water you drank needs enough time to rehydrate your muscles.

Please note that due to the nature of endurance training, with its very distinct energy and aerobic requirements, this particular eating protocol takes a markedly different approach from the other two. This shouldn't really come as a surprise, since each eating protocol is tailored to match particular exercise activities, with its own unique methods and strategies.

Meal Timing Schedule

All fat should be consumed in moderation, with total daily fat consumption not to exceed 25 to 30 percent of one's total intake. On non-workout days, carbs are allowable, and particularly encouraged in the form of vegetables and fruits, but please limit high-carb selections. Low-carb vegetables may be added to any snack or meal.

MEAL TIMING SCHEDULE

NON-WORKOUT DAY (REGULAR)

7 a.m.	Breakfast: lean protein + healthy fat + low-carb foods
10 a.m.	Snack: lean protein + healthy fats
12:30 p.m.	Lunch: lean protein + healthy fat + low-carb foods
3 p.m.	Snack: lean protein + healthy fats
5:30 p.m.	Dinner: lean protein + healthy fat + low-carb foods
7:30 p.m.	Snack: lean protein + healthy fat

NON-WORKOUT DAY (LOW ACTIVITY OR LEAN FOCUS)

7 a.m.	Breakfast: lean proteins + healthy fat + low-carb vegetables
10 a.m.	Snack: lean protein
12:30 p.m.	Lunch: lean-protein + healthy fat + low-carb vegetables
3 p.m.	Snack: lean protein
5:30 p.m.	Dinner: lean protein + healthy fat + low-carb vegetables
7:30 p.m.	Snack: lean protein

WORKOUT DAY

5 a.m.	Breakfast: lean protein + carbs
7 a.m.	Workout
10 a.m.	Recovery snack: protein + carbs
12:30 p.m.	Lunch: protein + carbs
3 p.m.	Snack: protein + carbs
5:30 p.m.	Dinner: protein + carbs
7:30 p.m.	Snack: protein + carbs

Goal III: Strength

Eating to Build Lean Muscle Mass

Essentially, muscles are built in the kitchen: Proteins are literally the building blocks of muscle and carbs are necessary for replenishing muscle glycogen. Together, they are a powerful combination to help muscle tissue repair itself and grow. This is why it's so very important for you to eat enough carbs and protein after exercising, ideally within 15 to 20 minutes after a workout to maximize muscle growth. Otherwise, you risk the breakdown of the very muscle tissue you've worked so hard to build through exercise and hopefully also through sensible, balanced nutrition.

Meal Timing Schedule

In a nutshell, here's how the program works: On non-workout days and for meals preceding workouts, stick to lean, high-protein foods and low-carb selections, preferably in the form of vegetables like cruciferous vegetables and leafy greens. On exercise days, eat high-protein, carb-rich foods after your workouts. Whenever possible, opt for nutrient-dense, carb-rich selections like fruit, whole grains, legumes, and squash; root vegetables like sweet potatoes should take precedence over foods of comparatively lesser nutritional value, i.e., "empty calories" like breads and pasta. Low-carb vegetables may be added to any snack or meal. All fat should be consumed in moderation, with total daily fat consumption not to exceed 25 to 30 percent of one's total intake.

MEAL TIMING SCHEDULE

NON-WORKOUT DAY

7 a.m.	Breakfast: lean protein + healthy fat
10 a.m.	Snack: lean protein + healthy fat
12:30 p.m.	Lunch: lean protein + healthy fat
3 p.m.	Snack: lean protein + healthy fat
5:30 p.m.	Dinner: lean protein + healthy fat
7:30 p.m.	Snack: lean protein + healthy fat

WORKOUT DAY

6 a.m.	Workout
7 a.m.	Breakfast or recovery shake: lean protein + carbs
10 a.m.	Snack: protein + carbs
12:30 p.m.	Lunch: protein + carbs
3 p.m.	Snack: protein + carbs
5:30 p.m.	Dinner: protein + carbs
7:30 p.m.	Snack: protein + carbs

WORKOUT DAY (ALTERNATE SCHEDULE)

5 a.m.	Breakfast: lean protein + healthy fat
7 a.m.	Workout
10 a.m.	Recovery snack: protein + carbs
12:30 p.m.	Lunch: protein + carbs
3 p.m.	Snack: protein + carbs
5:30 p.m.	Dinner: protein + carbs
7:30 p.m.	Snack: protein + carbs

The Meal Plans: Eat Like an Athlete

To help you meet your sports nutrition goals, below are the corresponding meal plans for each eating protocol—fat loss, endurance, and strength. See Part III for the recipes.

GOAL I: FAT LOSS	
DAY 1: EXERCISE DAY	
Pre-Exercise Meal	Beet Greens & Goat Cheese Omelet *(page 42)*
Post-Exercise Snack	Chocolate Raspberry Recovery Drink *(page 152)*
Post-Exercise Meal	Roasted Vegetable Pita Pizza *(page 100)*
Post-Exercise Snack	Olive Hummus *(page 134)* & Za'atar Crackers with Sesame, Cumin, Caraway, & Nigella Seeds *(page 138)*
Post-Exercise Meal	Piri Piri Chicken *(page 74)* and Portuguese Black Rice *(page 119)*
Post-Exercise Snack	Whipped Ricotta Cream with Fresh Berries *(page 135)*
DAY 2: OFF DAY	
Breakfast	Baked Egg in an Avocado with Pico de Gallo *(page 44)*
Snack	Rotolo di Tacchino al Forno (Turkey Florentine Mini Roulades) *(page 58)*
Lunch	Thai Vegetable Stir-Fry *(page 107)*
Snack	Sweet & Salty Peanut Butter Crunch Bars *(page 132)*
Dinner	Almond-Crusted Haddock *(page 66)* and Wilted Mustard Greens *(page 129)*
Snack	Lemonade with Fresh Mint & Lemon Slices *(page 154)*
DAY 3: EXERCISE DAY	
Pre-Exercise Meal	Samurai Salad (Wasabi Tuna Steak Salad) *(page 70)*
Post-Exercise Snack/Meal	Muscle-Building Protein Recovery Shake *(page 153)*
Post-Exercise Meal	Savory Noodle Kugel *(page 102)* and Tomato-Basil Soup with Greens *(page 52)*
Post-Exercise Snack	Baked Sweet Potato Chips *(page 130)*
Post-Exercise Meal	Chana Masala *(page 112)* and Pilau (Aromatic Basmati Rice) *(page 126)*
Post-Exercise Snack	Blueberry-Lemon Pots de Crème *(page 148)*

DAY 4: OFF DAY

Breakfast	Smoked Salmon Breakfast Sandwiches with Avocado & Goat Cheese *(page 45)*
Snack	Iced Coconut Chai Smoothie *(page 152)*
Lunch	Wild Mushroom Soup *(page 51)* and Italian-Style Turkey Breast with Fresh Herbs *(page 79)*
Snack	Hazelnut-Chocolate Mousse Pudding *(page 145)*
Dinner	Steakhouse-Style Pan-Seared Sirloin Steak *(page 86)* and Baby Arugula, Chickpea, & Hearts of Palm Salad *(page 56)*
Snack	Toasted Chili-Lime Pumpkin Seeds *(page 131)*

DAY 5: EXERCISE DAY

Pre-Exercise Meal	Tuna à la Tapenade with red pepper slices *(page 72)*
Post-Exercise Snack	Peanut Butter Truffle Smoothie *(page 155)*
Post-Exercise Meal	Cozze alla Marinara con Spaghetti (Mussels Marinara with Spaghetti) *(page 64)*
Post-Exercise Snack	No-Bake Chocolate-Cherry-Almond Energy Bites *(page 135)*
Post-Exercise Meal	Spicy Turkey Burgers *(page 75)* and Oven-Baked Rosemary-Parmesan Sweet Potato Fries *(page 116)*
Post-Exercise Snack	Popcorn Snack Bars *(page 136)*

GOAL II: ENDURANCE

DAY 1: EXERCISE DAY

Pre-Exercise Meal	Hot Quinoa Cereal with Nuts, Cinnamon, & Fresh Mango *(page 43)*
Post-Exercise Snack	Date & Almond Clusters *(page 131)*
Post-Exercise Meal	Buffalo Chili *(page 84)* with Roasted Butternut Squash & Corn *(page 128)*
Post-Exercise Snack	Guilt-Free Peanut Butter Fudge *(page 144)*
Post-Exercise Meal	Indian-Style Coconut-Ginger Shrimp Stir-Fry *(page 62)* with Pilau (Aromatic Basmati Rice) *(page 126)*
Post-Exercise Snack	Creamy Coconut Kheer (Indian Rice Pudding) *(page 140)*

DAY 2: OFF DAY

Breakfast	Huevos Rancheros *(page 46)*
Snack	Olive Hummus *(page 134)* and Tabouleh *(page 117)*
Lunch	Grilled Herbed Chicken *(page 78)* and Beet, Orange, & Fennel Salad *(page 54)*
Snack	Apricot-Papaya Pudding Parfait *(page 149)*
Dinner	Teriyaki Hamburgers with Wasabi-Avocado Sauce *(page 87)* and Asian-Style Jicama Slaw *(page 125)*
Snack	Badass Brownies with Chocolate Fudge Frosting & Raspberry Swirl *(page 142)*

DAY 3: EXERCISE DAY

Pre-Exercise Meal	Homemade Muesli *(page 38)*
Post-Exercise Snack	Chocolate Raspberry Recovery Drink *(page 152)*
Post-Exercise Meal	Southwestern Black Bean Salsa Tortilla Wrap *(page 98)*
Post-Exercise Snack	Popcorn Snack Bars *(page 136)*
Post-Exercise Meal	Spaghetti Squash & Spicy Meatballs *(page 90)*
Post-Exercise Snack	"Peaches & Cream" Frozen Fruit Bars *(page 150)*

DAY 4: OFF DAY

Breakfast	French Toast with Apricot Sauce *(page 48)*
Snack	Hazelnut-Chocolate Mousse Pudding *(page 145)*
Lunch	Fennel, Dill, & Black-Eyed Pea Soup *(page 53)* and Shrimp & Avocado Salad *(page 55)*
Snack	Coconut Oatmeal Rum Raisin Cookies *(page 151)*
Dinner	Grilled "Polenta-Style" Quinoa Cakes with Mushroom Ragù *(page 104)*
Snack	Pear & Pecan Clafouti *(page 150)*

DAY 5: EXERCISE DAY

Pre-Exercise Meal	Blueberry-Oatmeal Buttermilk Pancakes *(page 40)*
Post-Exercise Snack	Almond Butter–Frosted Almond & Date Muffins *(page 39)*
Post-Exercise Meal	Cold Sesame Noodles *(page 110)* with Pineapple-Ginger Stir-Fry *(page 118)*
Post-Exercise Snack	Healthy Homemade Trail Mix *(page 139)*
Post-Exercise Meal	Tequila-Lime Steak Fajitas *(page 88)* with Guacamole *(page 60)* and Refried Beans *(page 115)*
Post-Exercise Snack	Frozen "Banana Coconut Cream Pie" Custard *(page 148)*

GOAL III: STRENGTH

DAY 1: EXERCISE DAY

Pre-Exercise Meal	Beet Greens & Goat Cheese Omelet *(page 42)*
Post-Exercise Snack	Peanut Butter Truffle Smoothie *(page 155)*
Post-Exercise Meal	Grilled Vegetable Panini with Buffalo Mozzarella *(page 108)*
Post-Exercise Snack	Frozen "Banana Coconut Cream Pie" Custard *(page 148)*
Post-Exercise Meal	Poulet Amandine (Chicken with Almonds) *(page 82)* and Ginger-Garlic Baby Carrots *(page 123)*
Post-Exercise Snack	Whipped Ricotta Cream with Fresh Berries *(page 135)*

DAY 2: OFF DAY

Breakfast	Smoked Salmon Breakfast Sandwiches with Avocado & Goat Cheese *(page 45)*
Snack	Tuna à la Tapenade with red pepper slices *(page 72)*
Lunch	Zucchini "Fettuccine" Alfredo *(page 103)*
Snack	Hazelnut-Chocolate Mousse Pudding *(page 145)*
Dinner	Pan-Seared Scallops in Champagne Sauce *(page 67)* with Parmesan-Crusted Asparagus in White Truffle Oil *(page 114)*
Snack	Lemonade with Fresh Mint & Lemon Slices *(page 154)*

DAY 3: EXERCISE DAY

Pre-Exercise Meal	Iced Coconut Chai Smoothie *(page 152)*
Post-Exercise Snack	No-Bake Chocolate-Cherry-Almond Energy Bites *(page 135)*
Post-Exercise Meal	Cavatappi with Walnut-Almond Pesto & Sun-Dried Tomatoes *(page 101)*
Post-Exercise Snack	Blueberry-Lemon Pots de Crème *(page 148)*
Post-Exercise Meal	Crispy Southern Un-Fried Chicken *(page 81)* with Swoon-Worthy Sweet Potatoes *(page 129)*
Post-Exercise Snack	Mango Tart with Cardamom & Saffron *(page 146)*

DAY 4: OFF DAY

Breakfast	Baked Egg in an Avocado with Pico de Gallo *(page 44)*
Snack	Olive Hummus with crudités *(page 134)*
Lunch	Caribbean Stew *(page 69)*
Snack	Toasted Chili-Lime Pumpkin Seeds *(page 131)*
Dinner	Grilled Wild Salmon in Garlic-Dill Yogurt Sauce *(page 73)* and Cauliflower Mash with Rosemary & Roasted Garlic *(page 124)*
Snack	Sweet & Salty Peanut Butter Crunch Bars *(page 132)*

DAY 5: EXERCISE DAY

Pre-Exercise Meal	Greek-Style Eggplant Gratin with Feta & Tomato Sauce *(page 106)*
Post-Exercise Snack	Muscle-Building Protein Recovery Shake *(page 153)*
Post-Exercise Meal	Red Beans & Black Rice *(page 96)* with a side of Celery Rémoulade *(page 122)*
Post-Exercise Snack	Mexican Egg Salad spread onto crackers *(page 120)*
Post-Exercise Meal	Walnut & Parmesan–Crusted Chicken *(page 77)* and Kale-Potato-Leek Soup *(page 50)*
Post-Exercise Snack	"Peaches & Cream" Frozen Fruit Bars *(page 150)*

RECIPE EXCHANGE OPTIONS

The following recipes can be exchanged as *pre-exercise options* for the fat-burning and muscle-building meal plans and off-day options for all three meal plans:

- Sautéed Shrimp & Red Bell Peppers in Lemon-Garlic Sauce (page 61)
- Balsamic Chicken with Caramelized Onions (page 80)
- Coconut Chicken (page 76)
- Huanchinango Veracruzana (Red Snapper in Veracruz Sauce) (page 68)

The following recipes can be exchanged as *post-exercise options* for all three meal plans:

- Chocolate-Strawberry Waffles (page 49)
- Vegetable Quesadillas (page 57)
- Red Lentil & Garbanzo Bean Chili (page 92)
- Bulgur, Black Bean, & Feta Stuffed Peppers (page 94)
- Mushroom-Olive Quinoa Pilaf with Fresh Herbs (page 111)

PART III

LET'S GET COOKIN':
THE RECIPES

Breakfast

Homemade Muesli

Need to add some excitement to your breakfast routine? Then make your own muesli! It's not only yummy and nutritious, but it's also super quick and easy to make. Packed with fiber, quality protein and carbs, and omega-3s, this dish will give you the proper (and long-lasting) energy to start your day. Yield: 1 serving

⅓ cup rolled oats

2 tablespoons sliced almonds

1 teaspoon ground flaxseed

2 tablespoons no-sugar-added dried cherries (or if unavailable, raisins or chopped dates, etc.)

1 tablespoon pumpkin seeds

½ tablespoon chopped hazelnuts (or walnuts, if unavailable)

pinch of salt

1 teaspoon honey, or to taste (optional)

milk of choice, to serve

Combine all the ingredients in a bowl, mix thoroughly with a spoon, add milk (or nut or soy milk), and dig in!

Chef's Notes: No-sugar-added cherries can be found at Whole Foods Market or other similar health food or other grocery stores carrying organic, natural foods.

Almond Butter–Frosted Almond & Date Muffins

These make a great post-workout snack. Or, if you're in a rush, grab one for breakfast on your way out the door. Yield: 12 muffins

BATTER

1 cup whole pitted dates

½ cup boiling water

1¼ cups oat flour

1 teaspoon baking soda

¼ cup unsweetened soy milk

1 egg

1 teaspoon pure vanilla extract

¼ cup salted almond butter

½ cup honey

FROSTING

½ cup salted almond butter

¼ cup honey

MAKE THE MUFFINS: In a heatproof bowl, soak the dates in the boiling water for 10 minutes. Drain and allow to cool completely.

Preheat the oven to 350°F. Line the wells of a standard 12-cup muffin tin with paper liners. In a stand mixer fitted with the whisk attachment, combine the flour and baking soda on low speed until well-combined. In a food processor, combine the soaked dates, soy milk, egg, vanilla extract, almond butter, and honey, and pulse until completely smooth. Pour the wet ingredients into the bowl of the stand mixer and mix on low speed until fully incorporated.

Fill each muffin well to the top with batter. Bake for 20 to 25 minutes, or until a toothpick or knife inserted into a muffin comes out clean.

MAKE THE FROSTING: While muffins are baking combine the almond butter and honey in a food processor and pulse until smooth and creamy. Set aside. Remove muffins from oven and allow to cool on a wire rack for at least 10 to 15 minutes. Then use a spatula to spread frosting on each muffin. Serve warm.

Chef's Notes: Liquid and dry measuring tools will produce different amounts, so be sure to use them for their intended purpose. This is particularly important for baking, which relies upon the chemical reactions of a specific ratio of ingredients to yield the best results. This is why you might be able to wing it a bit when you're cooking, but baking requires precision.

Blueberry-Oatmeal Buttermilk Pancakes

This recipe provides a fun and tasty way to get in your daily fiber. The pancakes themselves are moist and warm with just the right amount of spice and vanilla. Not only are blueberries one of the highest sources of antioxidants, but they also provide the perfect flavor and texture contrast, and won't caramelize in the pan like some other fruits do. I love how they get all warm and gooey as they cook.

The surprising thing about this recipe is there's not a drop of butter in the batter and yet it still tastes really good. The secret is the low-fat buttermilk, which creates the proper thickness and adds some much-needed moisture.   Yield: 8 (3½ to 4-inch) pancakes

1 large egg, beaten

¾ cup low-fat buttermilk

1 teaspoon pure vanilla extract

1 tablespoon honey

1 cup rolled oats, finely ground into flour in a food processor

¼ cup unbleached all-purpose flour

1 teaspoon baking powder

1 teaspoon baking soda

¼ teaspoon salt

1 teaspoon ground cinnamon

⅛ teaspoon ground allspice

⅛ teaspoon ground cardamom

1 cup fresh (or frozen) blueberries

1 tablespoon (or less) unsalted butter, for lightly coating the pan

pure maple syrup or honey, to serve (optional)

PREPARE THE BATTER: In the bowl of a stand mixer fitted with the whisk attachment, whisk together the egg, buttermilk, vanilla, and honey on medium-high speed. In a medium bowl, stir together the ground oats, flour, baking powder, baking soda, salt, cinnamon, allspice, and cardamom until well combined. Add the dry ingredients to the wet ingredients, gently whisking on the lowest speed until just combined. Turn off the mixer and add the blueberries, gently folding them in by hand.

The batter should be fluid and thick, but not lumpy. Be careful not to make the batter too wet, because this'll make the pancakes harder to flip. For the best results, use a light touch and be careful not to overmix the batter or it'll be gluey and heavy, and will yield stiff, unpalatable pancakes.

MAKE THE PANCAKES: Heat a 12 or 13-inch nonstick sauté pan (or griddle) over medium-high heat until a drop of water sizzles when dropped on the surface. Once the butter has melted, turn the heat up to medium. Melt ½ tablespoon of butter in the pan, then turn down the heat to medium-low, quickly spreading the butter across the pan with a heatproof pastry brush. Working in batches, quickly but carefully ladle out batter, about ¼ cup at a time, tilting the pan so that the batter forms a thin layer (or spreading the batter with back of a spoon), and cook on medium heat for about 1 minute per side, or until small bubbles appear on the pancakes' surfaces and the undersides are golden brown. Repeat with the remaining batter until all the pancakes have been made. If necessary, melt and spread some of the remaining ½ tablespoon butter across the pan between batches each time until it's all used up. Try to fit as many pancakes as possible into the pan, while leaving yourself enough room to flip them, about ½ inch between pancakes.

Heat a plate in the microwave on high for about a minute. Stack the pancakes on the plate and cover them with a paper towel to keep them warm while you cook the remaining batter. Serve hot, with pure maple syrup or honey, if desired.

Chef's Notes: If you happen to make a few too many pancakes, not to worry; pancakes freeze well for future use. Allow them to fully cool, then store in a zip-top freezer bag. They can then be reheated in the oven, or even in the toaster oven if they aren't too large for it.

Please note that the amount of butter used is a very moderate amount. A little bit of butter is needed to cook the pancakes, as it's the key to creating crisp edges. It also helps to give them a nice golden brown color and, of course, adds a bit of richness to their overall flavor. It's better than using nonstick cooking spray, which is filled with harmful PFOAs (perfluorooctanoic acid) and other chemicals. Considering how healthy and low-fat the rest of the recipe ingredients are, a small amount of butter, in moderation, is perfectly fine. We're not encouraging you to eat a boring diet. It's important to enjoy your food while transforming yourself into a more fit and fabulous you. That way you'll be more likely to stick with a realistic way of eating that's harmonious with your mind, your taste buds, and your goals.

Beet Greens & Goat Cheese Omelet

Beet greens are probably one of the most underappreciated leafy greens. If you've never had them before, they taste a lot like spinach except they don't tend to absorb as much water, which is just perfect for an omelet. This is also why buttermilk is used in this recipe instead of milk. It gives omelets the proper amount of thickness and volume without adding too much moisture. Another ingredient in this recipe is walnut oil, which has been added for extra omega-3 content. Yield: 1 to 2 servings

3 eggs	2 tablespoon grated Parmesan cheese
¼ cup low-fat buttermilk	1 tablespoon fresh thyme leaves
1 tablespoon walnut oil	1 tablespoon finely minced fresh oregano leaves
¾ cup chopped beet greens (in bite-size pieces)	pinch of ground black pepper, or to taste
2 ounces goat cheese, crumbled	pinch of salt, or to taste

Beat together the eggs and buttermilk in a medium bowl and set aside. Heat the walnut oil in a large sauté pan over medium-high heat until glistening. Then quickly reduce the heat to low, add the chopped beet greens, and sauté for 3 to 5 minutes, or until tender. (The beet greens should sizzle when they hit the pan.) Pour in the egg mixture and allow to set, 1 to 2 minutes. Quickly sprinkle the goat and Parmesan cheeses over the omelet, followed by the herbs and spices, making sure to evenly distribute them across the pan. Using a spatula, lift up one side of the omelet and fold in half. Cook for 4 to 5 minutes per side. Serve and enjoy!

Chef's Notes: Low heat is the optimal level for a tender and well-cooked omelet. If the heat is any higher, the omelet will be dry and tough.

POWER TIP: EGGS

Eggs can also contain a high level of omega-3s, most typically in the form of ALA (alpha linolenic acid), although they may also be fortified with DHA (docosahexaenoic acid). However, these omega-3 levels depend upon what the hens are fed. Hens fed a diet of greens, insects, flaxseed, and/or fish oil will produce eggs with a much higher omega-3 content than hens that are fed corn or soybeans. The exact type of omega-3s found in eggs also depends upon the hens' diet as well. For example, when hens are fed fish oil, which contains DHA, this DHA makes its way into the eggs. Likewise, when hens are fed flaxseed, which contain ALA, a portion of this ALA is broken down into DHA and transferred to the egg yolks.

Hot Quinoa Cereal
with Nuts, Cinnamon, & Fresh Mango

At 24 grams of protein per cup, eating hot quinoa cereal is a tasty and effective way to get all nine essential amino acids the body needs for health and proper maintenance. It's for this reason that quinoa is considered a "complete protein." Be sure to soak the quinoa for at least 5 to 10 minutes before you cook it. Do not skip this important step, as soaking helps quinoa release its saponin, which creates a bitter taste unless removed.   Yield: 4 to 6 servings

QUINOA

5 cups water, divided

1 cup quinoa

1 teaspoon pure vanilla extract

¼ cup sliced almonds

¼ cup crushed walnuts

2 tablespoons honey, or to taste

1 tablespoon ground cinnamon

⅛ teaspoon salt

¾ cup soy or coconut milk (or skim milk, if you prefer)

1 cup mangoes, pitted, peeled, and diced

Bring 4 cups of the water to a rolling boil in a large covered pot. Meanwhile, soak the quinoa in the remaining cup of water for 5 to 10 minutes, until it starts to puff up a bit. (This is a very important step as quinoa needs to be soaked in order to release its saponin, which creates a bitter taste unless removed.) When the quinoa is ready, transfer it to a fine-mesh sieve, rinse under running water, and then drain and set aside.

Reduce the heat under the boiling water to low, then add the rinsed and drained quinoa into the pot, stir, cover, and simmer for 5 minutes. Uncover, add the vanilla, stir, cover again with the lid, and cook for a final 5 minutes.

While the cereal is cooking, spread the almonds and walnuts on an aluminum foil–covered toaster pan and toast on 350°F for 2 to 3 minutes, or until light golden brown. Watch carefully, as they will burn very easily. When finished, set aside to cool for 5 to 10 minutes. When the cereal is ready, uncover and stir in the honey, cinnamon, and salt. Fluff with a fork, then let stand another 5 minutes to cool slightly. Pour in the milk, then stir in the mango and toasted nuts. Serve in bowls.

Chef's Notes: Another great idea is to add raisins and/or other types of dried fruit (dried cherries, cranberries, etc.) to your hot cereal. Either incorporate separately or mix together with whatever fresh fruit you have on hand. Or add fresh coconut slivers or unsweetened shredded coconut, either in addition to or as a replacement for the almonds and walnuts.

Baked Egg in an Avocado with Pico de Gallo

Avocados are packed with healthy monounsaturated fats and vitamin A, which are particularly helpful for athletes. Vitamin A supports red blood cell formation and facilitates the transport of iron to your red blood cells, which helps oxygenate your blood, setting the stage to improve your VO2 max. The jalapeño in the pico de gallo adds a fair amount of heat. For less, use half the amount of diced jalapeño, or substitute it with 1 tablespoon diced green bell pepper. However, consuming chile peppers raises body temperature, which studies show may boost metabolism.   Yield: 1 to 2 servings

EGGS

1 Haas avocado, pitted, peeled, and halved

2 large eggs, at room temperature

salt and ground black pepper

PICO DE GALLO

1 extra-large vine-ripened tomato, diced and drained (about 1 cup)

2 tablespoons chopped scallions (about 1 large scallion)

1 tablespoon seeded, diced jalapeño pepper

1 tablespoon freshly squeezed lime juice

½ teaspoon mild Mexican chili powder

dash of salt

dash of ground black pepper

1 tablespoon finely minced fresh cilantro

MAKE THE EGGS: Preheat the oven (or a toaster oven) to 425°F. Using a spoon, scoop out a small amount of avocado from each avocado half. Nestle the avocado halves into a small baking dish so that they stay upright. Crack an egg into each avocado half, then season with salt and pepper to taste. Place the baking dish in the oven and bake for 20 to 25 minutes, or until cooked as desired.

MAKE THE PICO DE GALLO: While eggs are baking, combine all the ingredients in a large bowl. Stir to combine well and set aside. (Or, for faster prep, do this step in advance and then refrigerate the mixture in a covered container until serving time.)

Remove the baking dish from the oven and allow to cool for a few minutes before serving. Top each half with pico de gallo and serve.

Chef's Notes: It is very important that you do not cook the avocado for longer than 25 minutes or else it will taste bitter. You could say that the egg baking on top of the avocado acts as a kind of "heat shield." Haas avocados are one of the few kinds of avocados that can be cooked for a short time without being rendered inedible, so be sure to specifically use Haas avocados in this recipe.

Smoked Salmon Breakfast Sandwiches
with Avocado & Goat Cheese

Packed with omega-3s, protein, fiber, and heart-healthy monounsaturated fats, this dish makes for a nutritious but filling bite-size breakfast on the go. It's basically a healthier reimagining of the traditional "bagel and lox"—instead of nutritionally deficient bagel halves and cream cheese, there are now hydrating, electrolyte-rich cucumber slices and high-protein goat cheese (that's 6 grams of protein per ounce compared to only 2 grams of protein per ounce for cream cheese). The same texture and flavor juxtapositions are essentially preserved—creamy and crunchy, intense and mild—but without the empty starch-fest, extra saturated fat, and heavy bloated feeling. Yield: About 12 mini breakfast sandwiches

SPREAD

¼ cup goat cheese

1 tablespoon rinsed and drained capers

2 teaspoons freshly squeezed lemon juice

⅓ cup mashed avocado (a little less than ½ Haas avocado)

½ tablespoon finely minced fresh dill

SANDWICHES

1 large cucumber, sliced into 24 (¼-inch-thick) rounds

4 ounces high-quality smoked wild salmon, cut into small (1¼-inch) squares

MAKE THE SPREAD: Combine the ingredients in a food processor and pulse until creamy and fully incorporated. Set aside.

MAKE THE SANDWICHES: Lay half of the cucumber slices on a plate. Then top each slice with quarter-size dollop of spread, followed by salmon, and then a second cucumber slice. (Or, if you prefer open-faced sandwiches, simply omit the second cucumber slice.)

Chef's Notes: For an even quicker breakfast, make the spread in advance in a food processor and then chill it in the refrigerator. If you prefer to make the whole dish ahead of time, prepare the sandwiches and store them in the refrigerator in a tightly sealed container (or plastic wrap) for up to 3 days.

POWER TIP: CUCUMBERS

Cucumber has several properties that are of particular importance to athletes: It's rich in silica, which promotes joint health, and contains powerful antioxidants that help fight inflammation, as well as cancer.

Huevos Rancheros

Huevos rancheros, or "ranch-style" eggs, are considered to be one of the quintessential Mexican breakfasts. The dish's name came about because it was often served for brunch on rural farms, or ranchos. Of course, the popularity of this dish now extends well beyond its country of origin, and is commonly found as a breakfast or brunch selection on many Mexican restaurant menus. After you eat this meal, you'll probably be set for the entire day. Not only is it very filling and satisfying to eat, but it also covers all of the bases of a balanced meal: protein, carbs, a bit of fat, fiber, and more. It's breakfast, lunch, and dinner all rolled into one.   Yield: 4 servings

RANCHERO (TOMATO-CHILI) SAUCE

1 teaspoon extra-virgin olive oil

¼ cup finely diced yellow onion

1 teaspoon finely minced garlic (about ½ large clove)

1 tablespoon seeded, minced jalapeño pepper (about ½ jalapeño)

½ heaping cup finely diced vine-ripened tomatoes (about 1 small tomato)

2 tablespoons tomato paste

¼ teaspoon finely minced dried oregano

½ teaspoon ground cumin

pinch of ground cayenne pepper

pinch of ground black pepper

pinch of salt

½ tablespoon finely minced fresh cilantro

1 teaspoon freshly squeezed lime juice

TORTILLAS

4 small (5½-inch) low-fat soft corn tortillas

2 teaspoons extra-virgin olive oil, divided

¼ cup (2 ounces) shredded, tightly packed pepper Jack cheese

4 large eggs

ACCOMPANIMENTS

a few slices of avocado, or Guacamole (page 60)

¼ cup plain, nonfat Greek yogurt or low-fat sour cream

hot Refried Beans (page 115)

baked, lightly salted tortilla strips (made in oven while the tortillas are cooking)

MAKE THE RANCHERO SAUCE: Heat the olive oil over low heat in a medium saucepan. Add the onion, garlic, and jalapeño and cook, stirring, until tender, 4 to 5 minutes, stirring occasionally. Do not let the ingredients brown. Next add the tomatoes, tomato paste, oregano, cumin, cayenne, black pepper, and salt. Cook for another few minutes, stirring occasionally to prevent the ingredients from sticking to the bottom of the pan. Remove from the heat, transfer to a small serving bowl, mix in the cilantro and lime juice, and set aside.

MAKE THE TORTILLAS: Using a heatproof pastry brush, brush both sides of a tortilla with ¼ teaspoon olive oil, evenly distributing it in a thin layer, and then place into a large (12 to 13-inch) nonstick sauté pan on high heat, flipping the tortilla over every 10 seconds or so, several times, to create pockets of air bubbles in the tortilla. Turn the heat down to medium-high heat and then put the tortilla back in the pan, cooking on one side until golden brown, about 30 seconds. (While the tortilla is cooking, bubbles should start to form. This is normal.)

Transfer the cooked tortilla to a plate covered with a paper towel (to soak up any excess oil). Lift up the tortilla using a spatula and place it back into the pan, browned side up. Sprinkle 1 tablespoon of cheese on top and turn the heat down to low. The residual heat in the pan should melt the cheese and brown the tortilla. Cook just until the cheese starts to melt, about 2 minutes.

Then crack an egg into the pan beside the tortilla and continue to cook. Season with salt and pepper, to taste. If desired, flip the egg and make it over-easy. (If you're going to make the egg sunny-side up, then cover the pan with a lid, which helps to quickly steam the egg so it's not undercooked. You can also poach the egg if you prefer.) Then lift the egg up with a spatula and place on top of the tortilla. Remove from the heat and transfer to a plate. Top with the ranchero sauce, and, if desired, a few slices of avocado (or guacamole), a dollop of sour cream, a scoop of beans, and some baked corn tortilla strips.

Repeat with the remaining tortillas and eggs. Serve immediately.

Chef's Notes: If you'd like to reduce the amount of oil in this recipe even further, the tortillas can also be baked in the oven at 350°F for 20 to 25 minutes instead. Or, alternatively, tortillas can be placed between two paper towels and microwaved for about 15 seconds to soften them, before they are topped with a fried egg, ranchero sauce, and all the rest of the trimmings. If you are serving this recipe for two, I'd recommend making this dish in batches of two. Eat the first batch, and then return to the kitchen to make the second batch. The sauce can be made a day in advance and refrigerated overnight, then reheated before serving.

Variations: Traditional cheese selections for huevos rancheros include queso fresco, queso añejo, or queso blanco. If unavailable, the closest commercial substitutes would be mild feta cheese, Parmesan cheese, or Monterey Jack, respectively. Alternative choices include sharp cheddar, mozzarella, or farmer's cheese. Or, if you like, you can also use a blend of cheeses. If preferred, salsa verde could also be substituted for the ranchero sauce.

Tip: To speed up the cooking process, use two pans, one for each set of tortillas. They'll also be considerably warmer if cooked in this way. You can also enclose each completed serving in foil or place in the oven to keep warm.

French Toast with Apricot Sauce

This recipe puts a new—and much healthier—spin on an old breakfast classic. Coconut oil has a high smoke point and works well with the other flavor elements of this dish. Plus, it's a great source of immediately usable energy for athletes. The low-fat buttermilk gives the toast a light consistency while still keeping it relatively lean. Add cinnamon, nutmeg, and a hint of vanilla, and then drizzle some warm apricot sauce on top for a delicious start to your day! Yield: 4 servings

APRICOT SAUCE

¾ cup water

¼ cup no-sugar-added apricot preserves

½ tablespoon honey

1 teaspoon arrowroot powder or another thickening agent like cornstarch

½ teaspoon pure vanilla extract

½ teaspoon freshly squeezed lemon juice

TOAST

1 egg

¼ cup low-fat buttermilk (or if unavailable, use skim milk)

1 teaspoon honey

½ teaspoon pure vanilla extract

½ teaspoon ground cinnamon, plus more for sprinkling

pinch of ground nutmeg

pinch of salt, or to taste

1 tablespoon extra-virgin coconut oil, divided

4 slices whole-grain bread

MAKE THE APRICOT SAUCE: Place the water, apricot preserves, honey, and arrowroot powder in a small sauce pan. Stir thoroughly to combine, and bring to a boil over high heat. Reduce the heat to medium and cook until the honey is fully dissolved and the mixture has been reduced by half, 3 to 4 minutes, stirring occasionally. Stir in the vanilla and lemon juice. Remove from the heat and set aside to fully cool. Pour into a small syrup (or creamer) dispenser and set aside.

MAKE THE TOAST: Whisk together the egg, buttermilk, honey, vanilla, cinnamon, nutmeg, and salt in a deep, medium bowl. Heat the coconut oil in a large skillet until glistening, then reduce the heat to medium-low. While the oil is heating, dip the bread slices one at a time into the bowl, allowing them to soak for at least 1 minute per side to fully absorb the egg mixture before transferring them to the skillet. Place two slices in the pan and cook for 1½ to 2 minutes per side, or until golden brown. Repeat with the next 2 slices. Transfer the toast to 4 plates and serve immediately. Place a cinnamon shaker (or small custard dish of cinnamon) and the dispenser of apricot sauce on the table to allow your guests to top their toast according to their own preferences.

Chocolate-Strawberry Waffles

Not only are the flavors of strawberry and chocolate a natural complement to one another, but when you eat this dish, it'll almost feel like you're eating dessert instead of breakfast. Plus, the strawberries in this recipe get all oozy and warm when they're heated on the waffle iron. Simply delicious! Yield: 3 to 4 waffles

1 cup oat flour (if making yourself in a food processor, finely process 1¼ cups whole oats)

¼ cup ground flaxseed

1 teaspoon baking powder

1 teaspoon baking soda

⅛ teaspoon salt, or to taste

¼ cup unsweetened cocoa powder

1 teaspoon ground cinnamon

2 eggs

1 cup buttermilk

¼ cup honey

1 teaspoon pure vanilla extract

1 cup sliced, hulled fresh strawberries (a little less than 1 pint)

1 tablespoon extra-virgin coconut oil, for coating the waffle iron

Preheat the waffle iron. Add the oat flour, ground flaxseed, baking powder, baking soda, salt, cocoa, and cinnamon to a large electric mixing bowl. Mix on low speed, then slowly incorporate the liquid ingredients—eggs, buttermilk, honey, and vanilla—one by one, mixing until smooth. Turn off the mixer and fold in the strawberries with a spatula until just combined. Brush the waffle iron with coconut oil. Make the waffles in batches, pouring the mixture onto the hot waffle iron, closing the lid, and then cooking until golden brown. Top with additional sliced strawberries and desired condiments, and serve.

POWER TIP: COCONUT OIL

Despite the bad rap that coconut oil's gotten over the years, it's actually quite good for you when consumed in moderate amounts. First of all, let's address a myth: Not all saturated fats are bad for you. Two plant-based saturated fats, coconut and palm oil, in their natural and unadulterated forms, are among the few saturated fats that are healthy for you. They also help you to burn fat. These oils provide an immediately usable, sustainable source of energy, which makes them the perfect choice for athletes. When consumed in moderation, they create energy within the body, as opposed to most animal-based saturated fats, which have minimal health benefits and take a lot more energy to burn off.

So how can the saturated fat in coconut and palm oils be such an effective fat-burning mechanism? The answer lies in its biochemical composition, or more specifically, its atomic structure: Coconut oil contains lauric acid, a medium-chain triglyceride (MCT). Unlike the long-chain triglycerides found in other types of fats, MCTs have a shorter chain of carbon atoms and therefore can be more rapidly broken down (i.e., burned off) by the body and converted into energy. Since the body cannot readily store MCTs, it must burn them, thus resulting in an increase in fat oxidation (fat burning) and energy expenditure. This is how a moderate intake of coconut oil can lead to body fat loss.

Appetizers

Kale-Potato-Leek Soup

This soup has some amazing benefits for athletes: Its electrolytes and omega-3s are useful for post-exercise recovery, and its nutrients help maintain bone, cartilage, and cardiovascular health, as well as joint flexibility, metabolism, and hydration.   Yield: 4 (2-cup) servings

1 tablespoon extra-virgin olive oil

2 cups leeks, green parts only

1 tablespoon finely minced garlic (about 2 large cloves)

1 large fresh bay leaf

¼ cup dry sherry

4 cups water

3 cups chopped kale (including stems and center "ribs")

1 pound Yukon gold potatoes, peeled and diced (about 3 cups)

¼ cup finely minced fresh dill, tightly packed

2 tablespoons fresh Italian flat-leaf parsley, roughly chopped and tightly packed

1 tablespoon fresh thyme leaves, densely packed

½ tablespoon finely minced fresh rosemary leaves, tightly packed

¼ teaspoon salt, or to taste

⅛ teaspoon ground black pepper, or to taste

In a large sauce pot, warm the olive oil over low heat, then add the leeks, garlic, and bay leaf and sauté for 5 minutes. Deglaze the pan with the sherry, continuing to cook until the liquid is reduced by half. Add the water, increase the heat to medium-high, and bring to a boil. Then reduce the heat to low, add the kale and potatoes, cover with a lid, and simmer for 25 to 30 minutes, or until the potatoes are tender and easily pierced with a fork. Then add the dill, parsley, thyme, and rosemary, cover again, and simmer for 5 more minutes. Remove from the heat and allow to cool for 10 to 15 minutes. Discard the bay leaf. When almost completely cooled, transfer to a blender in batches and purée until smooth. Soup can be served hot or cold. Reheat over medium-low heat if needed.

Wild Mushroom Soup

This healthy version of mushroom soup still tastes rich and creamy, but without all of the fat. Enjoy! Yield: 2 servings

2½ cups fresh button mushrooms (8 ounces)

1¼ cups sliced mixed fresh mushrooms (like cremini, porcini, oyster mushrooms, etc.) (4 ounces)

1 tablespoon extra-virgin olive oil

½ yellow onion, finely minced

3 medium garlic cloves, minced

2 shallots, finely minced

⅓ cup sherry

1 tablespoon all-purpose flour

¼ teaspoon kosher salt, or to taste

1 teaspoon dried thyme

1 teaspoon dried parsley

½ teaspoon dried tarragon

4 cups water

⅔ cup plain, unsweetened soy milk

2 sprigs fresh thyme, for garnish

Soak all the mushrooms in a large bowl of lukewarm water for 15 to 20 minutes, then gently clean them under cold running water. Thinly slice the mushrooms and set aside.

In a large saucepan, warm the olive oil over medium-low heat. Add the onion, garlic, and shallots and sauté for 5 to 7 minutes, until softened but not browned. Stir occasionally to keep the ingredients from sticking to the bottom of the pan. To deglaze the pan, add the sherry and use a wooden spoon to loosen fond (the brown bits on the bottom of the pan). Continue to cook until only a thin layer of liquid is left. Whisk the in flour and combine thoroughly with other ingredients. Add the sliced mushrooms and season with the salt to help them cook faster and release their moisture. Add the dried thyme, parsley, and tarragon and stir thoroughly to combine. Cook the mushrooms for 10 to 15 minutes, stirring continuously. Add the water and cook for another 30 minutes or so. Let cool for several minutes and then pour into a blender with the soy milk. Gently pulse just a few times until the mushrooms have barely been chopped; the goal is to achieve a consistency that's a bit chunky so that the texture of the mushrooms can be fully appreciated. Pour into two bowls. Garnish each bowl with a sprig of thyme and serve.

Tomato-Basil Soup with Greens

Yield: 6 to 8 (2-cup) servings

1 tablespoon extra-virgin olive oil

¾ cup finely minced leeks, white parts only

½ cup finely minced shallots (3 large shallots)

1 large fresh bay leaf

¼ cup dry vermouth

12 cups water

3 cups diced vine-ripened tomatoes (about 4 large tomatoes)

½ cup tomato paste (almost a whole 6-ounce can)

1 teaspoon salt, or to taste

½ teaspoon ground black pepper, or to taste

4 cups chopped raw Swiss chard, in bite-size pieces

2 cups chopped raw kale, in bite-size pieces

1 cup raw baby spinach leaves

1 cup coarsely chopped fresh basil

¼ cup fresh marjoram leaves, coarsely chopped

¼ cup finely minced fresh flat-leaf parsley

1 tablespoon finely minced fresh oregano

⅜ to ½ cup (6 to 8 tablespoons) grated Parmesan cheese

In a large (6 to 8-quart) pot, heat the olive oil over medium-high heat until shimmering. Then reduce the heat to low and sauté the leeks, shallots, and bay leaf for 5 minutes on low heat, stirring occasionally. Deglaze the pan with the vermouth, and continue to cook until the liquid is reduced to a thin layer on the bottom of the pot.

Add the water, and bring to a rolling boil; cover the pot to help it boil faster. Add the tomatoes and tomato paste, and season with salt and pepper. Stir to combine and break up the tomato paste, cover, and cook for 10 minutes over medium heat. Then reduce the heat to low, remove the lid, add the chard, kale, spinach, marjoram, parsley, and oregano. Cover again and simmer for 5 to 6 more minutes. Remove from the heat, uncover, and allow to cool for 10 minutes. Discard the bay leaf, garnish each bowl with about 1 tablespoon Parmesan cheese, and serve immediately.

VARIATIONS: You can also add pasta, potatoes, and/or cannellini beans, if desired. To make this recipe vegan, simply omit the cheese, or use a non-dairy cheese substitute like soy cheese.

POWER TIP: KALE

Kale is a powerful leafy green that has some amazing benefits for athletes: It's high in the electrolyte calcium and omega-3s, both of which are useful for post-exercise recovery. Kale is also rich in iron, which is essential for oxygen transport, among other functions, and it also contains vitamins C and K, and various cancer-fighting antioxidants. The nutrients in kale help maintain bone, cartilage, and cardiovascular health, as well as joint flexibility, metabolism, and hydration.

Fennel, Dill, & Black-Eyed Pea Soup

Instead of discarding the stalks and fronds of a fennel bulb, use them to make this soup! Yield: 4 (2-cup) servings

1 tablespoon extra-virgin olive oil

1 cup diced yellow onion

1 tablespoon finely minced garlic (about 2 cloves)

¼ cup dry white wine (like Chardonnay)

3 cups coarsely chopped fennel stalks and fronds

8 cups water

1 (15.5-ounce) can black-eyed peas

¾ cup coarsely chopped fresh dill, tightly packed

¼ cup coarsely chopped flat-leaf parsley, tightly packed

¼ teaspoon ground black pepper, or to taste

½ teaspoon salt, or to taste

2 tablespoons freshly squeezed lemon juice

1 cup chopped tomatoes, for garnish (about ¼ cup per serving)

In a large stockpot, heat the olive oil over high heat until glistening, then reduce the heat to low, add the onions and garlic, and sauté for 5 minutes. To deglaze, add the white wine and stir to break up the fond (the brown bits on the bottom of the pan). Cook until the liquid has been reduced by half, then add the fennel stalks and fronds and cook for another 1 to 2 minutes.

Add the water, turn up the heat to high, and bring to a rolling boil. Then reduce the heat to low, add the black-eyed peas, and simmer, uncovered, for 15 to 20 minutes. Add the dill and parsley, season with salt and pepper, and simmer for 5 more minutes. Remove from the heat, let rest until almost fully cooled, stir in the lemon juice, and then transfer to a blender and blend, in batches, until smooth.

Ladle 2 cups of soup into each bowl and garnish with ¼ cup chopped tomatoes. Serve immediately. Leftover soup will keep for up 5 days in the refrigerator and up to 6 months or more in the freezer.

Beet, Orange, & Fennel Salad

This sophisticated, nutritious salad is a real people-pleaser, and it's quite filling too. Serve it for everyday meals, picnics, or parties.   Yield: 6 to 8 servings as an entrée, 10 to 12 servings as an appetizer

9 pounds beets with greens, unpeeled (about 3 large bunches)

¾ cup thinly sliced red onion

1 large fennel bulb, quartered and thinly sliced (about 2 cups)

2 large navel oranges, peeled and sliced into ¼-inch-thick rounds

1 tablespoon fresh thyme

2½ tablespoons red wine vinegar

3 tablespoons walnut oil

1 tablespoon finely minced garlic

⅛ cup finely minced shallot

¼ teaspoon Dijon mustard

⅛ teaspoon ground black pepper

⅛ teaspoon salt

⅛ cup dill, finely minced

4 ounces arugula

¼ cup crumbled goat cheese

While wearing latex or rubber gloves, slice off the beet greens from the beets on a nonporous cutting board and set aside. Bring a large covered pot of water to a rolling boil over high heat. Carefully add the beets to the pot using tongs to avoid backsplash. Boil for 25 to 30 minutes, or until tender when pierced with a fork. Remove from the heat. Drain the beets, then place them back into the pot to let them cool. When the beets are cool enough to handle, put on the gloves again and trim off the beet tips. Then rub off and discard their skins.

Slice the beets into ¼-inch-thick rounds and place into a large serving bowl along with the sliced onion, sliced fennel, and oranges. Place the thyme, vinegar, walnut oil, garlic, shallot, mustard, salt, and pepper in a food processor and pulse until smooth. Pour the dressing into the serving bowl, add the dill, and toss with the other ingredients until well-combined. Divide salad into equal portions. Place an equal amount of arugula onto each plate, then top with beet, orange, and fennel mixture. Sprinkle each portion with an equal amount of goat cheese and serve.

Chef's Notes: To keep the cutting board as dry as possible, slice the juiciest items last. The fennel would be first, then the garlic, shallots, red onions, beets, and finally, the navel oranges.

Shrimp & Avocado Salad

This is an ideal dish for picnics, barbecues, or festive summer parties. Please note that this recipe calls for cornichons, sour mini pickles. Be sure to get these rather than the sweet kind (gherkins).   Yield: 8 to 10 servings

MARINADE

¼ cup nonfat plain Greek yogurt

2 tablespoons freshly squeezed lemon juice

2 tablespoons Dijon mustard

1 tablespoon extra-virgin olive oil

1 tablespoon finely minced fresh dill, tightly packed

½ tablespoon finely minced fresh tarragon, tightly packed

½ teaspoon paprika

1 teaspoon garlic powder

¼ teaspoon ground black pepper

¼ teaspoon salt, or to taste

SALAD

1 pound cooked, peeled, deveined shrimp, cut into bite-size pieces (26 to 30 large shrimp)

½ cup diced red bell peppers (about ¼ large pepper)

½ cup diced orange bell peppers (about ¼ large pepper)

½ cup diced yellow bell peppers (about ¼ large pepper)

1 cup peeled, diced cucumber (about ½ large cucumber)

½ cup sliced scallions, white and green parts, into ¼-inch rounds

¼ cup finely diced celery (about ½ rib)

¼ cup finely diced cornichons, finely diced

1 cup avocado, peeled, pitted, and diced (about 1 Haas avocado)

MAKE THE MARINADE: In a medium bowl, thoroughly combine all the marinade ingredients.

MAKE THE SALAD: Add all of the salad ingredients except the avocados to the marinade. Toss until all the salad ingredients have been coated with dressing. Add avocados and gently combine until coated. Cover and refrigerate for a few hours to allow the flavors to meld. Serve cold or at room temperature.

Baby Arugula, Chickpea, & Hearts of Palm Salad

Not only is this salad super easy to make, but thanks to the chickpeas, which are packed with quality carbs and protein, this salad is deceptively filling and will give you enough energy to last for hours.   Yield: 4 servings as an entrée, 6 to 8 servings as a side dish

DRESSING

¼ cup extra-virgin olive oil

2 tablespoons freshly squeezed lemon juice

¼ teaspoon Dijon mustard

1 tablespoon finely minced fresh mint

½ tablespoon finely minced garlic (about 1 large clove)

⅛ teaspoon salt

⅛ teaspoon ground black pepper

SALAD

4 ounces baby arugula

1 (15-ounce) can chickpeas, drained and rinsed

1 (14-ounce) can hearts of palm, drained, rinsed, and sliced crosswise into ¼-inch rounds

½ cup grape tomatoes or diced vine-ripened tomatoes

¼ cup shaved Manchego cheese

MAKE THE DRESSING: Place all the dressing ingredients in a blender and pulse until creamy and smooth. Set aside.

MAKE THE SALAD: Place all the salad ingredients except the Manchego cheese in a large bowl. Drizzle on the dressing and thoroughly toss until all of the ingredients have been coated with dressing. Add the Manchego cheese and gently toss until combined. Serve and enjoy!

Vegetable Quesadillas

Packed with brightly colored vegetables, this dish is as pleasing to the eye as it is to the stomach. It makes a super-easy and nutritious go-to appetizer, dinner, or lunch. Quick and healthy, this dish can be prepared in a matter of minutes. It's got all the bases covered— it's high in protein, fiber, and quality carbs but low in fat, and it really satisfies. Yield: 4 servings

SALSA

½ cup diced vine-ripened tomato (about ½ medium tomato)

½ teaspoon dried cilantro

½ teaspoon dried oregano

½ teaspoon Mexican-style chili powder

⅛ teaspoon garlic powder

⅛ teaspoon onion powder

pinch of salt

1 scallion, white and green parts, sliced crosswise into ¼-inch rounds (about 2 tablespoons)

1 tablespoon seeded, diced jalapeño (about ½ jalapeño)

1 tablespoon freshly squeezed lime juice

QUESADILLA

1 large, low-fat whole wheat flour tortilla

1 teaspoon extra-virgin olive oil

⅓ cup low-fat shredded Monterey Jack cheese

¼ cup thinly sliced mushrooms

2 tablespoons finely diced red bell pepper

OPTIONAL TOPPINGS

½ Haas avocado, pitted, peeled, and thinly sliced (or prepared guacamole)

1 tablespoon finely minced fresh cilantro

2 tablespoons (or more) nonfat Greek yogurt (or sour cream)

Preheat the oven to 400°F.

MAKE THE SALSA: Place all the salsa ingredients in a bowl and mix until well combined. Set aside.

MAKE THE QUESADILLA: Place the tortilla onto a cookie sheet and brush with the olive oil. Flip over, then lift up on one side and fold in half to meet the other end. Lift top side and hold open while adding ingredients. Sprinkle the cheese onto the bottom half of the tortilla, followed by the salsa, and then the mushrooms and red bell pepper. Be sure to leave a ¼-inch border empty around the edge. Close the top of the tortilla, evenly pressing down on the tortilla all over using your fingers. Place into the oven and bake for 10 to 12 minutes, or until golden brown. Remove from the oven and carefully cut the quesadilla into quarters while still hot. (To ensure uniform portion sizes, first cut the quesadilla in half, and then cut those halves in half.) Transfer to a plate. Garnish with desired toppings and serve hot.

Rotolo di Tacchino al Forno
(Turkey Florentine Mini Roulades)

The inspiration for this recipe comes from Sicily. Rotolo *is an Italian word derived from the verb* rotolare, *which means "to roll." Italians also commonly refer to this dish as* involtini. *In English-speaking countries, "roulade" is the more commonly used term, which comes from the French word* rouler. *Although roulade can be made with a variety of meats, chicken and beef are probably most common. (When it's made with beef, it's typically referred to as* braciole.) *Turkey roulade is admittedly less common, but of course, it's a lot leaner than chicken.*

These mini roulades are the perfect finger food to serve as party hors d'œuvres. Even better, they can be made in advance and then either frozen or refrigerated for future use. Then all you have to do is reheat them just before serving. They can also be served cold or at room temperature.   Yield: About 50 mini roulades

FILLING

1 cup part-skim ricotta cheese

¼ cup grated Parmesan cheese

1 teaspoon freshly grated lemon zest

1 tablespoon freshly squeezed lemon juice

2 tablespoons slightly crushed roasted, salted pistachios

1 teaspoon paprika

½ teaspoon garlic powder

½ teaspoon onion powder

⅛ teaspoon ground black pepper

⅛ teaspoon salt, or to taste

pinch of ground nutmeg

¾ cup finely minced fresh baby spinach leaves, tightly packed

1 tablespoon finely minced flat-leaf parsley, tightly packed

1 tablespoon finely minced fresh basil, tightly packed

ROULADE

10 boneless, skinless turkey breast cutlets, in long strips (about 1¼ pounds)

½ cup ground flaxseed

⅛ teaspoon salt

1 tablespoon extra-virgin olive oil

At least 30 minutes before cooking, remove the turkey cutlets from the refrigerator and let them come to room temperature. Preheat the oven to 375°F.

MAKE THE FILLING: Using a spatula, thoroughly combine all the filling ingredients in a large bowl and set aside.

MAKE THE ROULADE: Spread a large sheet of waxed paper onto a clean surface; this will be used for prepping the cutlets. Place the ground flaxseed in a large shallow bowl, then dip a cutlet into the bowl, gently pressing the cutlet into the flaxseed to thoroughly coat it on both sides, and transfer onto the waxed paper. Repeat with the remaining cutlets until they have all been "breaded," spacing them evenly apart lengthwise on the baking sheet. Next, place about

2 tablespoons or more of the filling into the center of each cutlet, and using a knife (or your fingers), spread the mixture lengthwise along the cutlets, leaving about a 1-inch border on each end. Lifting up from the end that's closest to you, tightly roll up each cutlet away from you, taking special care to tuck the ends under. The finished product should resemble jelly rolls.

Transfer the roulades to a 7 x 11-inch glass baking dish, making sure to tightly nestle them next to one another to prevent them from unraveling. Season with the salt, sprinkling from a good distance above to evenly distribute. Drizzle with the olive oil to help brown the roulades.

Cover the baking dish with aluminum foil, and roast for about 25 minutes, or until the juices run clear and the meat is no longer pink on the inside. Then open the oven, pull out the rack with the baking dish, and remove the aluminum foil. Continue to bake for another 10 to 15 minutes, or until tender when pierced with a fork. Allow to cool for 10 minutes, then transfer to a large cutting board. With a sharp knife, cut the roulades crosswise into ¼ to ⅜-inch-thick rounds, about 5 rounds per roulade. Arrange on a large serving platter, providing toothpicks on the side, and serve warm or at room temperature.

These can be made a day in advance and refrigerated in a covered container.

Chef's Notes: While it's traditional to use metal poultry lacing pins and kitchen twine to lace together the roulades, in truth, you don't really need them, because the ingredients have a way of sealing together during cooking. In fact, I make roulades without using any twine at all and they stay in one piece, even during slicing. You just need a sharp knife and a firm but careful grip while you're slicing.

Guacamole

For less heat, be sure to use mild Mexican-style chili powder and just 1 teaspoon minced jalapeño. Serve with baked tortilla chips and salsa. Also makes a great addition to a sandwich, or a nice side for fish, chicken, or beef. Yield: 4 to 6 servings

3 large ripe avocados, halved, peeled, and pitted

2 tablespoons freshly squeezed lemon juice (from about 1 lemon)

2 tablespoons freshly squeezed lime juice (from about 1 lime)

1 teaspoon ground cumin

1 teaspoon Mexican-style chili powder

1 teaspoon dried oregano

⅛ teaspoon ground cayenne pepper

¼ teaspoon freshly ground black pepper

½ teaspoon kosher salt

2 scallions, white and green parts, sliced crosswise into thin rounds

2 teaspoons minced, seeded jalapeño

2 tablespoons finely minced cilantro

Scoop out the avocado flesh with a large spoon and place in a medium bowl, then immediately add the lemon and lime juices. Add the cumin, chili powder, oregano, cayenne, black pepper, and salt, and mash with a fork until just combined. The mixture should still retain a bit of its chunky texture. Add the scallions, jalapeño, and cilantro, mixing well after each addition. Serve immediately.

Chef's Notes: Avocado flesh oxidizes when it comes into contact with air. Lemon and lime juice will both help to delay this process. However, if you are storing the guacamole overnight, some discoloration may still appear the next day. The guacamole will still taste the same; simply mix it again to improve the color. This is why it's usually best to make guacamole within a few minutes of when you plan to serve it.

Entrées

Sautéed Shrimp & Red Bell Peppers
in Lemon-Garlic Sauce

Shrimp cooks fast, so it's perfect for those times when you're in a rush but still want to make a decent, healthy meal. This dish can be made in under 20 minutes flat, and that includes kitchen prep and cooking time. And by using precooked shrimp, the prep goes even faster. Feel free to use raw shrimp, if it's available to you. Yield: 2 servings

MARINADE

2 tablespoons extra-virgin olive oil

2 tablespoons freshly squeezed lemon juice

¼ teaspoon Dijon mustard

⅛ teaspoon ground black pepper

⅛ teaspoon salt

2 tablespoons fresh thyme

8 ounces cooked shrimp

SAUTÉ

1 tablespoon extra-virgin olive oil

¼ cup diced red onion

1 tablespoon finely minced garlic (about 2 cloves)

1 cup diced red bell pepper (about ¾ large pepper)

¼ cup chopped scallions, white and green parts, cut crosswise into ¼-inch rounds

¼ cup finely minced flat-leaf parsley

MAKE THE MARINADE: Whisk together the marinade ingredients in a small bowl. Place the shrimp in a plastic zip-top bag and pour in marinade. Seal and massage the marinade into the shrimp from the outside of the bag. Set aside to marinate for at least 1 hour. (For best results, marinate overnight.)

MAKE THE SAUTÉ: Heat 1 tablespoon extra-virgin olive oil in a large (12 to 13-inch) sauté pan until it glistens and sizzles. Then reduce the heat to low, add the onion, garlic, and red bell pepper, and cook until tender, about 5 minutes. Add the marinated shrimp and cook for 5 minutes more, stirring occasionally. Stir in the scallions and parsley, and cook for 5 more minutes. Serve and enjoy!

Indian-Style Coconut-Ginger Shrimp Stir-Fry

The spices and fresh curry leaves in this dish lend it a heady aroma and exquisite flavor, which pairs well with the ginger, garlic, and coconut flakes. And the real beauty of it all is that, for all of its complex flavor, this recipe is deceptively simple and quick to make. You'll find black mustard seeds at an Indian market or online.   Yield: 2 servings

¾ pound (12 ounces) medium shrimp, peeled and deveined

2 teaspoons black mustard seeds

½ teaspoon garam masala (recipe follows)

¼ teaspoon ground cayenne pepper

¼ teaspoon turmeric

¼ teaspoon ground mustard

½ teaspoon cumin seeds

⅛ teaspoon salt

1 tablespoon fresh curry leaves, chopped (about 8 fresh or 10 frozen large curry leaves)

⅛ cup unsweetened shredded coconut flakes

1 tablespoon freshly squeezed lemon juice

1 tablespoon extra-virgin coconut oil

1 tablespoon garlic, peeled and finely minced

½ tablespoon fresh ginger, peeled and grated (about ½-inch piece)

⅛ cup finely chopped scallions

mango chutney or green chutney, to serve

naan or rice, to serve (optional)

raita (Indian yogurt-cucumber sauce), to serve

Rinse the shrimp and pat them dry on paper towels. Add the black mustard, garam masala, cayenne, turmeric, mustard, cumin seeds, salt, and curry leaves to a large plastic zip-top bag and thoroughly combine. Add the shrimp, coconut flakes, and lemon juice in to the bag. Seal the bag and gently massage the spices and other ingredients into the shrimp from the outside of the bag to evenly coat the shrimp. Marinate in the refrigerator for at least 30 minutes (or for a zestier flavor, marinate overnight).

When you're ready to cook, allow the shrimp to reach room temperature while you heat the coconut oil in a large (12 to 13-inch) sauté pan over high heat until it glistens and sizzles. Reduce the heat to medium-low, then add the garlic and ginger, stirring continually. Sauté until the garlic is tender and the ginger no longer smells raw, 2 to 3 minutes. Add the marinated shrimp and cook, stirring often. If you're using raw shrimp, cook until the shrimp turn pink all over, about 1 minute. Add the scallions during the last 10 seconds of cooking, stirring occasionally. Serve hot, with mango or green chutney, naan or rice, and raita, if desired.

Chef's Notes: Even though the recipe calls for a minimum marinating time of 30 minutes, I recommend marinating the shrimp overnight. Of course, the longer you marinate the shrimp, the fuller the flavor. If so desired, you could also replace the shrimp with chicken to change things up. It would probably also be quite tasty with other types of seafood (like a white flaky fish, scallops, and crab) as well.

Garam Masala

Garam masala is an Indian spice blend readily available premixed at grocery stores, but making your own is so easy and more flavorful. Store any leftover amount in a tightly sealed container in a cool, dry place for future use.   Yield: 2 tablespoons

1½ teaspoons ground cumin

1½ teaspoons ground coriander

¾ teaspoon ground cardamom

½ teaspoon ground cinnamon

½ teaspoon ground ginger

½ teaspoon ground black pepper

pinch of ground clove

⅜ teaspoon finely crushed bay leaves

¼ teaspoon ground cayenne pepper (or to taste)

Mix all the ingredients together in a small bowl.

Cozze alla Marinara con Spaghetti
(Mussels Marinara with Spaghetti)

This dish is so simple to make, and yet, has a marvelously rich, full flavor. Not only that, but mussels are really good for you too! They're high in protein but low in fat and calories (per 3 ounces, they contain 70 calories and 1.9 grams of fat, 0.4 gram of which is saturated fat). They are a decent source of vitamin B12 as well as other B vitamins (especially folate), vitamin C, selenium, phosphorus, manganese, iron, and zinc. They are also rich in omega-3s. All of this delicious nutrition makes the enjoyment factor even greater. Yield: 8 servings as an entrée, and 10 to 12 servings as an appetizer

1 pound spaghetti (or other long or ribbon-cut pasta with a similar diameter)

1 tablespoon extra-virgin olive oil

½ cup diced yellow onion (about ¼ medium onion)

¼ cup minced shallot

1½ tablespoons finely minced garlic (about 3 large cloves)

1 large bay leaf (preferably fresh, if available)

2 cups good dry white wine, like Chardonnay or Orvieto, divided

1 (28-ounce) can crushed tomatoes

2 cups diced vine-ripened tomatoes (about 4 small tomatoes)

¼ cup tomato paste

¼ teaspoon salt

⅛ teaspoon ground black pepper

⅛ teaspoon red chile pepper flakes

2 tablespoons finely minced fresh oregano, tightly packed

1 tablespoon finely minced fresh marjoram, tightly packed

2 tablespoons finely minced fresh flat-leaf parsley, tightly packed

½ cup plus 2 tablespoons torn fresh basil, tightly packed, divided

2 pounds fresh mussels, scrubbed, rinsed, and debearded (about 85 small mussels)

½ cup grated or shaved Parmigiano-Reggiano cheese, for garnish

½ cup basil, tightly packed and torn into small pieces, for garnish

2 large lemons, cut into wedges, for garnish

Bring a large pot (8 to 10 cups) of salted water, seasoned with a few drops of olive oil, to a rolling boil. (Since there's a lot of water to boil, which will take a while, this is a good time to prep the ingredients for the marinara sauce.) Add the pasta and cook according to the package instructions until al dente. Drain into a colander, rinse with cold water, and drain again. Divide the pasta into equal portions, place in large, deep serving bowls with plates underneath, and set aside.

Heat the olive oil over high heat in a large (5 to 6-quart) pot until it sizzles and glistens. Reduce the heat to low and add the onions, shallots, and garlic, and bay leaf, and sauté until tender, about 5 minutes, stirring frequently. Deglaze the pan with 1 cup of the wine, stirring to break up the fond (the brown bits on the bottom of the pan). Then stir in the crushed tomatoes, vine-ripened tomatoes, and tomato paste until the tomato paste has been adequately broken up and the mixture is thoroughly blended. Cook for about another 5 minutes, and continue to stir on occasion to keep the sauce from sticking to the bottom and burning.

Add the remaining 1 cup of wine and increase the heat to high. Season with salt, black pepper, and red chile pepper flakes. When the broth has come to a boil, add the fresh the herbs in order—first the oregano, followed by the marjoram, parsley, and basil—so that the hardier herbs cook a bit longer. Then immediately add the mussels and quickly cover with a tight-fitting lid. Allow the mussels to steam for exactly 5 minutes. Set your kitchen timer, so that you don't forget about them. (It's very important to cook them for exactly 5 minutes; any longer and the mussels will overcook and taste quite unpleasant.)

Immediately after the timer goes off, carefully remove the lid while wearing heatproof oven mitts that fully cover your hands and wrists, and position the rest of your body a good distance away from the rising steam. Remove the pot from the heat and discard any unopened mussels (see note). Using a slotted spoon, scoop them into the large bowls containing the pasta, 10 to 11 mussels per person. Pour equal amounts of sauce over the top of each bowl. Sprinkle each portion with 1 tablespoon Parmigiano-Reggiano cheese and 1 tablespoon basil. Garnish each plate with a lemon wedge and serve immediately.

If you wish, you can make the sauce a few days in advance. When you're ready to cook the mussels, just bring the marinara sauce to a boil, followed by the mussels, cover with a tight-fitting lid, and cook for the requisite 5 minutes.

Chef's Notes: Important: For health and safety reasons, mussels should always be alive before they're cooked. Otherwise, you might become severely ill. This is why it's important to only use closed mussels. However, after having said that, please be aware that sometimes the open ones are still alive and just need a little bit of prodding to get them to "wake up" and close again. So if any open while you're preparing them (they will often open when rinsed), just give them a few gentle taps with the back of a knife or a spoon to see if they close. If not, discard them. Also discard any ones with broken shells. For more on mussel preparation, see page 156.

POWER TIP: PARMESAN

Parmesan has a high level of calcium, which helps the body burn off fat after meals, in turn boosting your metabolism. Here's how: Calcium acts as a messenger for various hormones like calcitonin, salcatonin, and parathroid hormone (PTH), which help metabolize calcium in the body. This process is called calcium homeostasis. When sufficient calcium levels are maintained in the body, there's no need for the body to release these hormones to regulate calcium levels, which allows for a higher rate of fat oxidation.

Almond-Crusted Haddock

For the best results, purchase the haddock fillets as two long, wide ½-pound pieces. Look for fish that have been filleted with uniform thickness for even cooking. Yield: 4 servings

1 cup sliced almonds

½ cup finely minced fresh flat-leaf parsley, tightly packed

2 tablespoons finely minced fresh oregano, tightly packed

3 tablespoons fresh thyme, tightly packed

2 tablespoons finely minced fresh rosemary, tightly packed

⅛ teaspoon salt

⅛ teaspoon ground black pepper

2 eggs, lightly beaten

2 (8-ounce) haddock fillets, skins intact

1 tablespoon extra-virgin olive oil

2 tablespoons finely minced shallots (about 1 small shallot)

2 tablespoons finely minced fresh garlic (about 4 large cloves)

1 large bay leaf

¼ cup dry white wine, like Chardonnay

2 tablespoons freshly squeezed lemon juice

Preheat the oven to 350°F and line a rimmed baking sheet with aluminum foil. Spread the almonds on the baking sheet and toast in the oven until light golden brown, about 1 minute. Watch carefully, as nuts tend to toast very quickly, and you don't want to end up with charred cinders. Let the almonds cool fully. Evenly spread the almonds onto a cutting board and cover with plastic wrap. Use the flat, smooth side of a meat mallet to pound the almonds into uniform little pieces. The almonds should only be crushed, not pulverized into oblivion.

Transfer the cooled almonds to a large plastic zip-top bag along with the parsley, oregano, thyme, rosemary, salt, pepper, and eggs. Seal and shake the bag until well-combined. One at a time, place each fish fillet into the egg mixture and then into the bag and gently shake to coat. Do not dry the fish; the moisture is needed to bind the spices and nuts to the fish. Set aside on a baking sheet lined with parchment paper.

Heat the olive oil over high heat in a large (12 to 13-inch) sauté pan until glistening. Reduce the heat to low, add the shallots, garlic, and bay leaf, and sauté for 5 minutes, or until tender. Deglaze with white wine, stirring to loosen the fond (brown bits on the bottom of the pan), cooking until the liquid is reduced by half.

Using a large spatula, transfer the fish fillets to the pan and grill for 4 minutes per side. When the fish starts to turn a light golden brown, test for doneness with a fork or knife. The flesh should be soft and flaky. Using 2 spatulas if necessary, transfer the whole fish fillets from the pan to a nonporous cutting surface. Use a sharp knife to cut each fillet in 2. Transfer to plates and let rest for at least 5 minutes before serving. Squeeze a little lemon juice on top of each fillet and serve.

Pan-Seared Scallops in Champagne Sauce

This quick, no-fuss recipe proves that you don't have to spend forever and a day slaving over a hot stove in order to produce a delicious and nutritious meal. The great thing about scallops is that they only take a total of 6 to 8 minutes to cook, which is welcome news for busy athletes.

You can get a lot of flavor from a healthy, simple preparation if you just know how to make the most of your ingredients. Dishes don't have to be fattening or complicated in order to taste good. For instance, while most champagne sauces contain cream and butter, this version is much lighter and instead relies upon the freshness of its ingredients for its vibrant flavor.

This dish is delicious atop a bed of asparagus or spinach.   Yield: 2 servings of 4 to 5 scallops each

1 tablespoon extra-virgin olive oil

2 tablespoons finely minced shallot (about 1 small shallot)

1 tablespoon finely minced garlic (about 2 large cloves)

¼ cup Champagne or other dry good-quality sparkling white wine

¼ cup low-sodium chicken stock

1 tablespoon arrowroot powder or other thickening agent

⅛ teaspoon Dijon mustard

¾ teaspoon finely minced fresh rosemary

½ teaspoon chopped fresh thyme leaves

⅛ teaspoon finely minced fresh tarragon

⅛ teaspoon salt

⅛ teaspoon ground black pepper

½ pound large, fresh diver-caught sea scallops, cleaned (8 to 10 large scallops)

½ teaspoon freshly squeezed lemon juice

½ tablespoon finely minced fresh flat-leaf parsley, finely minced

1 tablespoon minced fresh chives

Heat the olive oil in a large (12 to 13-inch) sauté pan over high heat until glistening. Reduce the heat to low, add the shallots and garlic, and sauté until tender, about 5 minutes. Turn up the heat to medium and immediately deglaze with the Champagne and chicken stock, stirring to break up the fond (the brown bits) from the bottom and sides of the pan. Add the vegetable broth, then stir in the arrowroot powder and mustard. Continue to cook until the liquid's volume has been reduced by half and the sauce begins to thicken. Stir in the thyme, tarragon, salt, and black pepper, then turn up the heat to medium-high.

Pat the scallops dry with a paper towel and add them to the pan, lightly searing them on both sides until golden brown, 3 to 4 minutes per side. Remove from the heat, let cool for 1 to 2 minutes, then stir in the lemon juice and parsley. Divide into 2 equal portions, pour the remaining sauce over the top, then garnish each serving with ½ tablespoon chives. Serve immediately.

Huanchinango Veracruzana (Red Snapper in Veracruz Sauce)

Yield: 2 servings

SNAPPER

2 (4 to 6-ounce) red snapper fillets

⅓ cup plain almond meal

¼ teaspoon dried oregano

1 tablespoon olive oil

SAUCE

1 (14.5-ounce) can diced tomatoes with their juices

½ cup diced vine-ripened tomato (about 1 small tomato)

1 tablespoon finely minced garlic

¼ cup diced yellow onion

1 ounce julienne-cut sun-dried tomatoes (not packed in oil)

½ tablespoon seeded, diced jalapeño pepper

10 Greek olives, pitted and diced

2 teaspoons capers, rinsed and drained

1 tablespoon freshly squeezed lemon juice

1 tablespoon finely minced fresh flat-leaf parsley

MAKE THE SNAPPER: Gently wash the fish fillets and lay on a plate. Do not dry; the moisture is needed in order for the almond meal to stick to the fish. Combine the almond meal and dried oregano in a large plastic zip-top bag. Seal and shake to combine. Lightly bread fillets by placing them in the bag one at a time, then sealing and gently shaking the bag to coat each fillet. Set aside.

Heat the olive oil over high heat in a large (12 to 13-inch) sauté pan until glistening, tilting the pan around to evenly distribute. Reduce the heat to medium and then add breaded fish fillets. Sauté the fish for 1 minute per side and then put the fish back on the plate. (Do not cook the fish all the way through at this point.)

MAKE THE SAUCE: Add the canned diced tomatoes (including their juices), fresh diced vine-ripened tomatoes, garlic, and onion to the sauté pan the fish was cooked in. Cook for 3 to 5 minutes, or until the liquid is reduced by about half. Then add all the remaining sauce ingredients to the pan, making sure that the sun-dried tomatoes have been submerged in the tomato juice. Cook for about another minute. If necessary, add a small amount of water to the pan to keep the ingredients from burning and/or sticking to the bottom of the pan. Clear a space for the fish fillets, and then add them back to the pan one at a time. Each time you add a fillet into the pan, cover it with sauce to keep it moist and make room for all of the ingredients. Cook for 2 to 3 more minutes per side, or until the fish is tender and flaky when pierced with a fork. Red snapper cooks very quickly, so be sure to watch the fish very carefully so that you don't overcook it. Remove from the heat and serve.

Caribbean Stew

In place of the cod in this recipe, you can also use another firm, non-flaky white fish like monkfish, mahi mahi, haddock, or halibut. This dish is especially delicious served with a side of Swoon-Worthy Sweet Potatoes (page 129).   Yield: About 6 (2-cup) servings

2 tablespoons extra-virgin coconut oil, divided

1 pound cod fillets, skinned and cut into bite-sized pieces

½ cup finely minced shallot (about 2 large shallots)

2 tablespoons finely minced garlic (about 4 large cloves)

2 tablespoons fresh ginger, peeled and finely minced (from about one 2-inch piece)

½ cup diced celery

1 large fresh bay leaf

6 cups water

1 (13.5-ounce) can coconut milk

3 cups diced vine-ripened tomatoes (about 7 large tomatoes)

6 tablespoons tomato paste

1 tablespoon seeded, diced Scotch Bonnet chile (about 1 small chile)

1 cup diced red bell pepper (about ¾ large pepper)

1 cup diced green bell pepper (about ¾ large pepper)

1 cup sliced okra, cut crosswise into ¼-inch rounds

¼ teaspoon ground allspice

1 teaspoon saffron threads

¼ teaspoon ground black pepper, or to taste

½ teaspoon salt, or to taste

½ tablespoon fresh thyme leaves

2 tablespoons freshly squeezed lime juice

¼ cup finely minced fresh cilantro

In a large (12 to 13-inch) sauté pan, heat 1 tablespoon of the coconut oil over high heat until shimmering. Reduce the heat to medium-high, then add the cod fillet pieces and sauté 5 minutes per side, or until crisp and golden brown.

Meanwhile, in a large stockpot, heat the remaining 1 tablespoon coconut oil over high heat until shimmering. Reduce the heat to low, then add the shallots, garlic, ginger, celery, and bay leaf, and sauté for 5 minutes, or until tender, stirring occasionally. Deglaze with ¼ cup of the water, stir to loosen the fond (the brown bits on the bottom of the pan), then add the remaining 5¾ cups water and the coconut milk and bring to a rolling boil, covering with a lid to boil faster. Reduce the heat to medium-low, stir in the tomatoes and tomato paste, and simmer, uncovered, for 10 minutes. Add the sautéed cod pieces, Scotch Bonnet chile, red and green bell peppers, okra, allspice, saffron, pepper, salt, and thyme leaves. Then cover again, and simmer for 5 to 7 more minutes, or until the vegetables are tender but still retain their color. Remove from the heat, uncover, and allow to cool for 10 minutes. Discard the bay leaf, add lime juice, stir, and adjust the seasoning with salt and pepper to taste. Garnish with fresh cilantro, and serve immediately.

Samurai Salad (Wasabi Tuna Steak Salad)

Tuna is an excellent source of lean, muscle-building protein, with 25 grams of protein per 3-ounce serving. Yield: 4 servings

MARINADE

6 tablespoons sesame oil

2 tablespoons freshly squeezed lime juice

2 tablespoons soy sauce

½ teaspoon wasabi paste

2 teaspoons ground ginger

2 teaspoons garlic powder

¼ teaspoon kosher salt

½ teaspoon coarsely ground black pepper

2 tablespoons sesame seeds

SALAD

1 pound very fresh tuna steak, cut into 1-inch-thick cubes

1 ripe medium Haas avocado, peeled, pitted, and cut into bite-size pieces

¼ cup sliced scallions, white and green parts, cut crosswise into ⅛-inch rounds (about 4 scallions)

½ cup diced red onion

¼ cup coarsely chopped cilantro leaves

1 heart of romaine lettuce, chopped into bite-size pieces

¾ cup diced red bell peppers (about ½ large pepper)

¼ cup shredded carrots (about ¼ large carrot)

¾ cup sliced cucumber, peel scored vertically with the tines of a fork and then sliced crosswise into ¼-inch-thick rounds

SALAD DRESSING

¼ cup sesame oil

2 tablespoons soy sauce

2 tablespoons freshly squeezed lime juice

1 tablespoon water

1 tablespoon honey

1 teaspoon ground ginger

1 teaspoon garlic powder

¼ teaspoon ground mustard

½ tablespoon sesame seeds

⅛ teaspoon ground black pepper

MAKE THE MARINADE: Combine all the marinade ingredients in a small bowl and whisk together until emulsified.

MAKE THE SALAD: Add the tuna cubes to a plastic zip-top bag along with the marinade, and seal the bag. Massage the marinade into the tuna from the outside of the bag until well-coated. Let rest on the countertop until the tuna reaches room temperature, 20 to 30 minutes.

In the meantime, place the remaining salad ingredients in a large salad bowl and toss.

Place a large wok or stir-fry pan over high heat; make sure the pan is very hot before adding the tuna. Place the tuna cubes in the pan and cook for only 30 seconds per side. (Cover the pan with a splatter screen to avoid getting zinged with bursts of crackling, sizzling hot oil.) Set them aside on a plate to cool, then transfer them to the salad bowl.

MAKE THE SALAD DRESSING: Whisk all the dressing ingredients together in a small bowl. When the tuna is cool, drizzle the salad with salad dressing, and gently toss. Serve and enjoy!

Chef's Notes: Both the marinade and the salad dressing can be made in advance to save time. To avoid cross-contamination, be sure to wash your hands after handling raw fish.

To find out more information about which species of tuna are ecologically safe to eat, please consult the Environmental Defense Fund's Seafood Selector, seafood.edf.org.

POWER TIP: AVOCADOS AND ATHLETES

Unless you've been living under a rock for the last couple of years, you've probably already seen 5 zillion articles plastered all over the web and other forms of media about how the avocado is one of the world's most amazing superfoods. Avocados are particularly rich in healthy monounsaturated fats and vitamin A, both of which have a myriad number of health benefits, and many of them are of particular use to athletes. For starters, Vitamin A supports muscle tissue growth by helping to create essential proteins in the body. It also helps boost testosterone, which plays a key role in increasing muscle mass and bone density. Vitamin A also has another athletic benefit: It helps oxygenate your blood by supporting red blood cell formation and transporting iron to your red blood cells. And of course, if you're trying to improve your VO2 max (how much oxygen your body is able to consume and use while exercising), you'll want to take full advantage of this benefit.

Tuna à la Tapenade

Want to pack on lean muscle mass and reduce post-exercise inflammation? Then try this tasty, easy-to-make, no-cook dish, which is made with no mayonnaise and is simply chock-full of lean protein and omega-3s. Tapenade is a refreshing, not to mention much healthier, alternative to mayo. It not only keeps the tuna moist, but also gives it a lighter texture and much more flavorful taste as well. Yield: 6 to 8 servings

TAPENADE

2 large garlic cloves, unpeeled

1 cup Greek olives, pitted (about 18 large olives)

1 tablespoon capers, soaked in ¼ cup water for 10 minutes, and then drained

½ tablespoon freshly squeezed lemon juice

1 tablespoon extra-virgin olive oil

¼ teaspoon Dijon mustard

1 tablespoon finely minced fresh flat-leaf parsley

½ teaspoon dried oregano

½ teaspoon dried crushed rosemary

½ teaspoon dried marjoram

½ teaspoon dried basil

½ teaspoon dried thyme

⅛ teaspoon red chili pepper flakes

⅛ teaspoon ground black pepper

TUNA

2 (12-ounce) cans tuna in water, drained

⅔ cup pitted and chopped Greek olives (about 14 large olives)

1 tablespoon finely minced fresh flat-leaf parsley

4 red bell peppers cut into long strips

MAKE THE TAPENADE: Wrap the unpeeled garlic cloves in aluminum foil and roast at 400°F in a toaster oven for 10 minutes. While the garlic is roasting, prep all the other tapenade ingredients and place them into the food processor. Unwrap and peel the garlic, let cool for a few minutes, then add to the food processor. Pulse until smooth and set aside.

MAKE THE TUNA: Place drained tuna in a large, nonporous bowl. Add the tapenade to the bowl using a spatula, followed by the ⅔ cup chopped Greek olives and 1 tablespoon finely minced parsley, and thoroughly combine. Divide into equal portions and serve with red bell pepper strips on the side. The red pepper strips can conveniently double as "utensils" to spoon the tuna-tapenade salad right into your mouth. If desired, place the tuna-tapenade mixture and red bell peppers on top of a salad or use as a sandwich filling.

Grilled Wild Salmon
in Garlic-Dill Yogurt Sauce

Lean and luscious, this dish is marinated in a mild, tangy sauce that allows the salmon's flavor and flaky, tender texture to shine through. Be sure to buy wild-caught salmon rather than farmed-raised; wild salmon has a much higher omega-3 content, not to mention much less exposure to disease, antibiotics, pesticides, and artificial additives. Yield: 4 servings

MARINADE

3 tablespoons low-sodium soy sauce

1 cup yogurt

2 teaspoons Dijon mustard

½ cup dried dill seeds

juice of 1 lemon (2 to 3 tablespoons)

1 tablespoon grated lemon zest

1 teaspoon ground ginger

2 teaspoons ground cumin

½ teaspoon black pepper

½ teaspoon salt

½ tablespoon garlic powder

SALMON

4 (4-ounce) salmon steaks, about 1 inch thick, with skin intact

¼ cup rinsed and drained capers, for garnish

MAKE THE MARINADE: Add the marinade ingredients to a large plastic zip-top bag and mix well using a spoon.

MAKE THE SALMON: Place the salmon steaks into the bag and thoroughly coat them with the marinade by gently massaging it into the fish from outside of bag. Refrigerate overnight to marinate, or for at least 3 to 4 hours, before grilling.

About 30 minutes before cooking, remove the salmon from the refrigerator and set it aside. (This allows the fish to reach room temperature to ensure even heat distribution during cooking.) Heat a grill to medium heat. Grill the salmon, with the lid closed, for 4 to 5 minutes per side (see note). Garnish the salmon with capers and serve.

Chef's Notes: The best way to ensure perfectly cooked salmon is to set a timer to help you keep tabs on the fish and then check it to see whether it needs a few more minutes. To test for doneness, place a knife into the flesh of the salmon and pry it open to see how pink the flesh is on the inside. (I personally like mine to be a medium pink color; tender, but not too fleshy.) When the salmon flesh flakes with a knife or fork, it's done. Be sure to remove the salmon just as it reaches the flaking point, or it will begin to dry and toughen. Perfectly done salmon is tender, moist, and flaky on the inside. For more on perfect salmon every time, see page 157.

Piri Piri Chicken

Piri piri means "pepper pepper" in Swahili, which describes both the dish itself and the African pepper traditionally used to make it. The piri piri chile pepper was apparently so incendiary that it seems they needed to repeat the word "piri" twice when naming it to underscore their point. Since this particular pepper is hard to find in the U.S., this recipe calls for red Thai chilies. For less heat, use only 2 or 3 chiles. Serve with Portuguese Rice (page 119).   Yield: 4 (8-ounce) servings

2 pounds bone-in, skin-on chicken wings, breasts, thighs, and drumsticks (should be about 2 of each)

1 cup extra-virgin olive oil, plus additional for brushing

3 tablespoons coarsely chopped shallot (about 1 large shallot)

4 tablespoons coarsely chopped garlic (about 8 large cloves)

¼ cup peeled and finely minced fresh ginger (about a 4-inch piece)

4 large red Thai (bird's eye) chile peppers, minced (about 1 heaping tablespoon)

½ cup coarsely chopped fresh cilantro

1 tablespoon fresh oregano leaves

¾ cup freshly squeezed lemon juice

¼ cup red wine vinegar

4 tablespoons paprika

2 teaspoons coarse kosher salt (or to taste)

2 teaspoons ground black pepper

1 teaspoon ground cayenne pepper (optional, for extra heat)

The night before you plan to serve the chicken, remove it from the refrigerator. On a nonporous cutting board, score the chicken all over with a sharp knife, slicing past the skin and into the surface of the flesh, and set aside. (This will allow the marinade to penetrate the chicken meat for a fuller flavor.) Combine all the remaining ingredients in a food processor and process until smooth. Using tongs, place the chicken into a large plastic zip-top bag, followed by the piri piri sauce, reserving about 1½ cups for basting the chicken during grilling. From the outside of the bag, massage the sauce all over the chicken, making sure to work it into every crack and crevice. Store the reserved sauce in an airtight container. Refrigerate both the chicken and the reserved sauce overnight.

About 30 minutes before serving, remove the chicken from the refrigerator to allow it to reach room temperature. Preheat an outdoor grill to medium-high heat. Place the chicken pieces onto the grill and baste all over with ¾ cup piri piri sauce. Close the grill top, and grill for 10 to 15 minutes, flip the chicken pieces over and baste with the remaining ¾ cup sauce. Close the grill top and cook for another 10 to 15 minutes, or until the juices run clear and the meat is no longer pink on the inside when pierced with a fork.

Spicy Turkey Burgers

Turkey burgers make an incredibly lean meal. For full, moist flavor, I recommend using ground turkey, which is typically 93 percent lean. If you'd like to go even leaner, you can use ground turkey breast, which is 99 percent lean, but be careful not to overcook it, as it can easily become dry if cooked for too long.   Yield: Makes 4 burgers

BURGERS

1 tablespoon paprika

1 tablespoon garlic powder

1 tablespoon ground cumin

2 teaspoons ground oregano

2 teaspoons ground coriander

1 teaspoon ground ginger

½ teaspoon ground dry mustard

½ teaspoon ground cloves

½ teaspoon ground allspice

1 teaspoon ground chipotle pepper or ½ teaspoon cayenne pepper, or to taste

¼ teaspoon ground black pepper, or to taste

½ teaspoon salt, or to taste

¼ cup low-sodium soy sauce

¼ teaspoon Worcestershire sauce

1⅓ pounds lean ground turkey

ACCOMPANIMENTS

4 whole wheat, multi-grain, or sesame hamburger buns, halved and toasted if desired

thinly sliced red onions (1 onion slice per burger)

sliced tomatoes (1 tomato slice per burger)

lettuce (1 large leaf per burger)

thinly sliced avocado (1 to 3 small slices per burger)

In a large bowl, mix together the paprika, garlic powder, cumin, oregano, coriander, ginger, dry mustard, cloves, allspice, chipotle or cayenne, black pepper, and salt with your hands until the ingredients are evenly distributed. Add the soy sauce, Worcestershire sauce, and ground turkey, and mix thoroughly.

Shape the turkey meat mixture into 4 (3½ to 4-inch) patties using either your hands or a hamburger patty maker. Let the meat reach room temperature before cooking.

Before you turn on the grill, lightly oil the grill grate so that the patties don't stick to it. Grill the patties for 5 to 7 minutes total over medium heat, until browned on the outside and the center is no longer pink. Cook through to the desired level of doneness. Simultaneously toast the hamburger buns on the grill, if desired. Serve burgers on buns with desired accompaniments.

Chef's Notes: So why use 1⅓ pounds and not 1 pound of ground turkey? Well, first, a lot of ground turkey comes packaged in ⅓-pound amounts. Second, ⅓-pound is the perfect amount to fill a hamburger patty maker 4 times for 4 decent-sized burgers, whereas 1 pound divided into 4 portions just isn't quite enough meat to make a satisfying burger that's just the right size for the eyes and the stomach.

Coconut Chicken

Coconut makes almost anything taste good. It tastes great in seafood dishes (particularly with fish and shrimp), snacks, and all sorts of desserts and beverages. This recipe uses coconut flakes, coconut milk, and coconut oil, so it's got lots of coconut flavor. When creating delectable crusts for meat and seafood dishes, coconut flakes make a great substitute for bread crumbs, not to mention the fact that they've got a much greater nutritional value as well. Plus, in this particular recipe, the golden brown, crunchy coconut crust is not only tasty and nutritious, but also has a practical culinary purpose as well—it helps seal in moisture to keep the chicken tender and juicy. Yield: 2 servings

2 (4-ounce) boneless, skinless chicken breast fillets

1 tablespoon Garam Masala (page 63)

1 teaspoon ground coriander

½ teaspoon garlic powder

⅛ teaspoon salt

¼ cup unsweetened, shredded or grated coconut flakes

¼ cup coconut milk

1 tablespoon coconut oil

1 tablespoon finely minced fresh cilantro leaves, tightly packed, for garnish

About a half hour before cooking time, remove the chicken from the refrigerator and let rest until it's reached room temperature.

Thoroughly combine the garam masala, coriander, garlic powder, and salt in a wide but shallow bowl. Then add the coconut flakes and mix well. Set aside. Pour the coconut milk into a separate bowl with the same dimensions. Place a large (12 to 13-inch) sauté pan over high heat for about 60 seconds. Then reduce the heat to medium-low and add the coconut oil. Next, quickly dip each fillet, one at a time, into the bowl of coconut milk, shake to remove the excess, then dip into the coconut flake mixture. Gently press the chicken into the mixture to completely coat on both sides, and then place into the pan. The chicken should sizzle when it hits the pan; if not, the pan isn't hot enough. Cook 4 to 5 minutes total, or until the juices run clear and the meat is no longer pink on the inside when pierced with a fork. Garnish each portion with cilantro to serve.

Chef's Notes: Remember that the meat will continue to cook while it's resting on the plate (the temperature will rise by a few degrees), so be sure to cook the chicken just until the pink disappears and it's no longer fleshy. Otherwise, you risk overcooking it, and nothing's worse than dry, tough chicken.

Walnut & Parmesan–Crusted Chicken

Not only is this dish low in saturated fat, but the ingredients have some amazing health properties, which are of particular significance to athletes. Parmesan is one of the highest-protein, naturally low-fat cheeses there is. It's important to feed your muscle lean protein, especially right after exercise, to help it repair and grow. Walnuts and flaxseeds are chock full of omega-3s, which help reduce post-exercise inflammation. Chicken contains the highest amount of valine of any food. Valine is one of the essential branched chain amino acids (BCAAs) that help build muscle. The fresh herbs in this dish contain phytonutrients, which contain beneficial antioxidants. Yield: 2 servings

2 (4-ounce) boneless, skinless chicken breast fillets

½ cup walnut pieces

¼ cup ground flaxseed

½ cup grated Parmesan cheese

1 tablespoon fresh marjoram

1 tablespoon fresh thyme

½ tablespoon fresh oregano

⅛ teaspoon onion powder

⅛ teaspoon garlic powder

⅛ teaspoon salt

¼ teaspoon ground black pepper

1 large egg, at room temperature

1 tablespoon freshly squeezed lemon juice

A half hour before cooking, remove the chicken from the refrigerator and allow it to reach room temperature. Set aside.

Add all the remaining ingredients except the egg and lemon juice to a food processor and pulse until finely ground. Transfer to a large, shallow bowl and set aside. Crack the egg into another large shallow bowl, add the lemon juice, and beat together. Set aside.

Heat a large (12 to 13-inch) sauté pan on high for 30 seconds. Then reduce the heat to medium-low. Dip the chicken fillets one at a time into the egg mixture, shaking off any excess, and then transfer them to the bowl with the walnut-cheese mixture, coating the chicken with crumbs on all sides and pressing to adhere. Be sure to wash off your hands between each dipping to make the chicken easier to handle. Place the chicken fillets into the pan. The chicken should sizzle as it hits the pan; if not, the pan isn't hot enough. Sauté the chicken for 5 to 6 minutes per side, or until golden brown and the juices run clear. (You might have to adjust the cooking time slightly, depending upon thickness.) Cut into the chicken with a fork and knife to test for doneness. The chicken should be juicy but no longer pink or fleshy on the inside. Remove from the heat and place onto plates. Let rest for a few minutes before serving. (The meat will continue to cook as it rests, so be sure not to overcook it.)

Chef's Notes: To make this dish Paleo, simply omit the salt, Parmesan, and flaxseed. Also, if you'd like to experiment by substituting other types of nuts, I suggest trying almond slivers, pecans, or macadamia nuts, all of which will complement this dish rather nicely.

Grilled Herbed Chicken

This dish is great for barbecues and outdoor picnics, and it's super quick and easy to make, too. If incorrectly cooked, grilled chicken can end up dry, chewy, and unappetizing. See page 157 for tips on grilling tender, juicy chicken.   Yield: 4 servings

1 (3-pound) package bone-in, skin-on 8-piece cut chicken (4 breasts, 2 drumsticks, 2 wings)

¼ cup finely minced fresh sage, tightly packed

¼ cup finely minced fresh oregano, tightly packed

¼ cup finely minced fresh thyme, tightly packed

2 tablespoons freshly squeezed lemon juice

½ cup extra-virgin olive oil

¼ teaspoon salt, or to taste

¼ teaspoon ground black pepper, or to taste

3 tablespoons paprika

Poke holes all over the chicken with a sharp knife. Be sure to pierce the skin deeply, so that the seasoning will enter and be fully absorbed by the meat. Next place the chicken into a large plastic zip-top bag followed by all of the remaining ingredients and seal. Massage the marinade into the chicken from the outside of the bag. Make sure to rub the marinade into all of the cracks and crevices so that it fully penetrates the meat. Marinate in the refrigerator overnight.

At least 30 minutes before serving, remove the chicken from the refrigerator and let rest in order for it to reach room temperature. This will ensure even heat distribution when grilling. Preheat the grill to high heat. Reduce the heat to medium and carefully place the chicken pieces on the grill grate, evenly spacing them apart so that they do not touch. (If you are grilling with gas or charcoal, be especially careful when placing the chicken onto the grill, as the flames will very likely kick up when the marinade drips through the grates.) Use tongs when grasping and maneuvering the chicken and stand back a good distance from the grill when placing the chicken onto it. Close the grill lid. Set the timer to 15 minutes. After about 10 minutes, open the grill lid and check on the chicken, cutting into it with a knife and fork to check on its progress. At around the 15-minute mark, the chicken should be ready to be flipped to the other side. Reduce the heat to medium-low and close the grill lid once more. Set the timer for about 12 minutes. (The grill will be very hot and so the second side will cook a lot faster.) Check for doneness after about 12 minutes. Cook until the juices run clear when the chicken is pierced with a fork. Transfer to a serving tray. Let the chicken rest for at least 5 minutes before serving.

Italian-Style Turkey Breast with Fresh Herbs

Serve this dish with steamed vegetables for a satisfying meal. Yield: 4 servings

2 tablespoons olive oil

1 tablespoon finely minced garlic

¼ cup dry white wine, like Chardonnay

1 pound thinly sliced skinless turkey breast fillets

2 tablespoons minced fresh rosemary

2 teaspoons dried marjoram leaves

1 tablespoon paprika

¼ teaspoon ground black pepper

¼ teaspoon salt

Heat the olive oil in a large (12 to 13-inch) sauté pan over medium-high heat until glistening, then reduce the heat to low, add the garlic, and sauté for 5 minutes or until tender, stirring frequently. Deglaze with white wine, stirring to release the fond (the brown bits from the bottom of the pan) and turn up the heat to medium-low. Add the turkey and rosemary, season with the marjoram, paprika, pepper, and salt, and cook for 3 to 4 minutes per side, or until golden brown.

Balsamic Chicken with Caramelized Onions

This dish has a rather bold, pronounced flavor, so it's best served with simple accompaniments like steamed vegetables and/or a baked sweet potato. Yield: 2 servings

8 ounces boneless, skinless chicken cutlets, rinsed and defatted

½ cup balsamic vinegar, divided

1 tablespoon minced garlic (about 2 large cloves)

2 tablespoons finely minced fresh flat-leaf parsley, tightly packed

1 tablespoon finely minced fresh rosemary leaves, tightly packed (about 2 sprigs)

½ teaspoon dried oregano leaves

½ teaspoon dried thyme leaves

⅛ teaspoon salt

⅛ teaspoon ground black pepper

1 tablespoon extra-virgin olive oil

1 cup red onion, peeled, halved, and sliced into ¼-inch crescent slivers (about ½ medium onion)

Wash the chicken cutlets and lay them on a nonporous cutting board or other smooth, clean surface. Cover the chicken with plastic wrap and tenderize by pounding flat with the bumpy (waffle-patterned) side of a meat mallet to a uniform thickness of about ¼ inch. After the chicken has been tenderized, cut each piece into halves (or long strips, if you prefer). Place cutlets into a zip-top plastic bag, followed by ¼ cup of the balsamic vinegar, garlic, parsley, rosemary, oregano, thyme, salt, and pepper. Seal the bag and massage the spices into the chicken from the outside of the bag. Marinate overnight, or for at least 4 to 6 hours, in the refrigerator.

In a large sauté pan, warm the olive oil over medium-low heat, then sauté the onions until browned around the edges, about 10 minutes. Deglaze with the remaining ¼ cup balsamic vinegar and continue to cook until the liquid is reduced to a thin layer on the bottom of the pan.

Push the onions to one side of the pan or, if necessary, temporarily remove them to make more room for the chicken; it's important not to crowd the pan so that the chicken pieces cook evenly. Remove the marinated chicken from the refrigerator, and transfer the contents of the zip-top bag into the sauté pan. Cook the chicken for about 3 minutes on each side, or until golden brown. Be sure to scrape off the fond (the brown, caramelized bits) from the bottom of the pan and place it on top of the chicken and onions. Remove from the heat and serve immediately.

Crispy Southern Un-Fried Chicken

To keep the chicken meat moist and low-fat, this recipe calls for yogurt instead of oil. It's also oven-baked instead of fried. See page 157 for important tips on working with raw chicken.   Yield: 4 to 5 servings

CHICKEN

10 chicken drumsticks (about 4 pounds), with skin intact, rinsed, defatted, and patted dry

1 cup plain, nonfat Greek yogurt

1 tablespoon white distilled vinegar

1 tablespoon ice water

BREADING

1 cup dried plain bread crumbs

1 cup almond meal

1½ tablespoons onion powder

1 tablespoon paprika

1 tablespoon dried thyme

1 tablespoon dried basil

1 tablespoon dried oregano

2 teaspoons garlic powder

2 teaspoons dried parsley

2 teaspoons salt, or to taste

1 teaspoon ground sage

½ teaspoon dried marjoram

½ teaspoon ground black pepper

¼ teaspoon ground cayenne pepper

PREPARE THE CHICKEN: Keep the chicken in the refrigerator until it's ready to be prepped and baked. It's very important that both the chicken and the yogurt stay very cold, which helps the breading adhere to the chicken and contributes to its crispy texture. (If necessary, you can prep the chicken in an ice bath before working with it, in order to keep it super-cold.)

Preheat the oven to 400°F. Cover a large baking tray with aluminum foil (for easy clean-up) and set aside. Thoroughly combine the yogurt, vinegar, and ice water in a medium bowl. Cover and refrigerate ready to used.

MAKE THE BREADING: Pour all of the breading ingredients into a large plastic zip-top bag, seal tightly, and shake vigorously to combine. Remove the yogurt mixture and the chicken from the refrigerator. Roll each piece of chicken in the yogurt mixture and then transfer it, one piece at a time, into the plastic bag containing the breading mixture, shake to thoroughly coat, and then place it on the baking tray. Repeat until all the pieces have been breaded.

Place the baking sheet on the bottom shelf of the oven and bake for 1 hour, or until the juices run clear and the flesh is no longer pink, turning the pieces every 20 minutes (with tongs) to allow for even browning. Serve hot or at room temperature.

Chef's Notes: If you prefer, use a pastry brush to apply the yogurt mixture, which helps to control the amount of coating you use and is also good for wiping off any excess. The yogurt coating shouldn't be excessively thick.

Poulet Amandine (Chicken with Almonds)

"Amandine," sometimes misspelled as "almondine," is a French culinary term meaning "prepared or garnished with almonds." The almonds in this preparation can be sliced, slivered, flaked, or whole. Fish and green beans are most commonly served amandine, although chicken is another popular option. This recipe is a much healthier version than the typical amandine. Serve with quinoa, couscous, or rice. Yield: 2 servings

8 ounces boneless, skinless chicken breasts, rinsed, defatted, tendons removed, and patted dry

⅛ teaspoon salt, or to taste

⅛ teaspoon ground black pepper

1 tablespoon extra-virgin olive oil

¼ cup finely minced shallots (about 1 large shallot)

1 tablespoon finely minced garlic (about 2 large cloves)

1 large fresh bay leaf

½ cup dry white wine (like Chardonnay), divided

1 tablespoon very finely minced fresh Tuscan Blue rosemary leaves (or other mild rosemary), tightly packed

1 tablespoon very finely minced fresh oregano, tightly packed

1 tablespoon very finely minced fresh marjoram leaves, tightly packed

¼ cup fresh finely minced basil leaves, tightly packed

2 tablespoons blanched slivered almonds

½ tablespoon freshly squeezed lemon juice

Remove the chicken from the refrigerator 30 to 45 minutes before you plan to start cooking, so that it reaches room temperature. This helps ensure even cooking.

Next, place the prepared chicken breasts onto a clean, nonporous surface and cut into 2-inch-wide strips. Cover with plastic wrap and tenderize, pounding with the bumpy, textured end of a meat mallet until ⅛ inch thick. Discard the plastic wrap. Season the chicken with salt and pepper. Set aside.

Heat the olive oil in a large (12 to 13-inch) sauté pan over high heat. Reduce the heat to low and add the shallot, garlic, and bay leaf, and sauté until tender, about 5 minutes. Stir occasionally. Deglaze with ¼ cup of the white wine, stirring to loosen the fond (the brown bits on the bottom of the pan). Simmer until the liquid is reduced so there's only a thin layer on the bottom of the pan before adding the chicken.

Transfer the chicken to the pan, spacing the pieces far enough apart so as not to crowd the pan. Add the rosemary, oregano, marjoram, basil, and almonds. Cook the chicken for about 2 to 3 minutes per side, or until the chicken is no longer pink, its juices run clear, and its exterior has turned golden brown on both sides. While the chicken is cooking, add the remaining ¼ cup white wine to prevent the chicken from burning or sticking to the bottom of the pan. Watch the pan carefully, as tenderized chicken doesn't take very long to cook through and brown. Lower the heat even further if the chicken starts to burn.

When ready, remove from the heat, discard the bay leaf, and pour the lemon juice over the chicken. Divide into equal portions. Transfer to plates and serve immediately.

Gin & Ginger Chicken

Tenderized chicken cooks much faster because it's thinner and has more exposed surface area after it's been tenderized.   Yield: 2 servings

8 ounces boneless, skinless chicken breasts, well-rinsed, trimmed of fat, and patted dry

1 tablespoon sesame oil

½ cup finely minced shallot (about 1 large shallot)

⅓ cup chopped scallions, white and green parts (7 to 8 small scallions)

⅓ cup celery, diced (about 1 small stalk)

1 tablespoon peeled, finely minced fresh ginger (about a 1-inch piece)

1 large fresh bay leaf

1 tablespoon low-sodium soy sauce

1 cup dry, distilled gin (or if unavailable, use tequila)

½ teaspoon Chinese five-spice powder

⅛ teaspoon salt

⅛ teaspoon red chile pepper flakes

1 teaspoon freshly squeezed lime juice

½ teaspoon sesame seeds

1 tablespoon coarsely chopped fresh cilantro

Lay the prepared chicken cutlets on a nonporous cutting board or other smooth, clean surface. Cover with plastic wrap, and tenderize the chicken by pounding flat with the bumpy, textured side of meat mallet to a uniform thickness of about ¼ inch. After the chicken has been tenderized, cut each piece crosswise into thirds (or smaller, if desired).

Heat the sesame seed oil in a large (12 to 13-inch) nonstick sauté pan over high heat until glistening. Reduce the heat to low, then add the shallots, scallions, celery, ginger, and bay leaf, and sauté for about 5 minutes, until tender. Turn up the heat to medium-high and add the soy sauce and chicken. Cook the chicken until golden brown and slightly crispy around the edges (but still moist and tender on the inside), about 3 minutes per side. Deglaze the pan with gin, scraping off the fond (brown bits) from the bottom of the pan as the liquid evaporates. Quickly stir in the five-spice powder, salt, and red chile pepper flakes, and reduce until the liquid is only a thin layer on the bottom of the pan. When ready, remove from the heat and squeeze the lime juice over the chicken. Discard the bay leaf. Divide into 2 equal portions and transfer to plates. Sprinkle each portion with sesame seeds, garnish with fresh chopped cilantro, and serve.

Buffalo Chili

This flavorful, lean chili recipe is so easy, you virtually can't mess it up! Take it with you to work or eat it for dinner. It's not only portable, but also takes well to freezing and reheating. It's a real no-brainer! These days, buffalo meat is relatively easy to find. It's carried in a lot of generic supermarkets, so you won't necessarily have to go trotting off to a specialty store to find it. Yield: 8 to 10 servings if made with the olives, about 6 to 8 servings without

1 pound ground buffalo meat

2 tablespoons ground cumin

2 tablespoons paprika

1 tablespoon ground coriander

½ tablespoon Mexican-style chili powder (mild)

⅛ teaspoon ground cayenne pepper, or to taste

½ teaspoon salt, or to taste

1 tablespoon finely minced fresh oregano, tightly packed, or 1 teaspoon dried oregano

1 tablespoon extra-virgin olive oil

1 large bay leaf

1 tablespoon finely minced garlic (about 2 large cloves)

1½ cups diced yellow onion (about 1 small onion)

1½ cups diced green bell pepper (about 1 large bell pepper)

1½ cups diced red bell pepper (about 1 large pepper)

1 (28-ounce) can crushed tomatoes

14 ounces water (fill empty crushed tomatoes can halfway with water)

1 (6-ounce) can tomato paste

1 tablespoon apple cider vinegar

1 (15.5-ounce) can black beans, drained and rinsed

1 (15.5-ounce) can kidney beans, drained and rinsed

1 (15.5-ounce) can California olives, pitted and sliced crosswise into ¼-inch rounds (optional)

¼ cup cilantro (or more), finely minced, for garnish

Thirty minutes before serving, remove meat from refrigerator and let rest to reach room temperature. This allows for even heat distribution during cooking. Next, thoroughly combine the cumin, paprika, coriander, chili powder, cayenne pepper, salt, and fresh oregano in a small bowl and set aside.

In a large, wide stockpot, sear the meat over high heat for about 10 minutes, or until completely browned all the way through, stirring frequently and breaking up the meat into small pieces using a heatproof spatula. Remove from the heat. Drain the liquid fat from the pot, transfer the meat to a bowl, and set aside. Thoroughly clean the pot and return to the stove.

Heat the olive oil over high heat until glistening. Then reduce the heat to low and sauté the bay leaf, garlic, and onions for 5 minutes or until tender, stirring occasionally. Next, add the meat back in, then the green and red bell peppers, followed by the crushed tomatoes, water, tomato paste, vinegar, black beans, kidney beans, and reserved spice mix, and stir. Simmer for about 15 minutes, or until the peppers are just cooked enough so that they still retain their color and a bit of crunch. Let cool for about 10 minutes, then stir in the olives, if using. Discard the bay leaf and serve, garnished with cilantro.

POWER TIP: BUFFALO MEAT

Buffalo/bison meat is naturally lean, and, if eaten as part of a regular diet, has also been shown to reduce LDL (bad) cholesterol. It's also much higher in protein, iron, omega-3s, and amino acids than beef is. Even better, buffalo are naturally disease-resistant and grow faster than domestic animals, which means that producers will typically raise them as naturally as possible, that is, without antibiotics and growth hormones. In fact, many of the unnatural—and very unhealthy!—techniques used to increase cattle (and other domestic livestock) production thankfully do not work for bison. Bison demonstrate what most of us have already known all along to be true: When it comes to our food supply, the less mucking around with Mother Nature, the better for both the animals and for our own health. If you've never had buffalo before, you'll probably be pleased to know that it doesn't taste gamey at all, nor does it have a strong flavor or aftertaste. It's really quite pleasant to eat. I would advise, however, that just as you would do with other lean cuts of meat like London broil or turkey breast, you pay close attention to cooking times for buffalo, as it can dry out if it's cooked for too long.

Steakhouse-Style Pan-Seared Sirloin Steak

Seasoned in a delectable spice rub packed with flavor and then cooked until juicy and tender, this steak preparation is lean and deceptively simple. If tip-side sirloin steaks are unavailable, substitute another lean cut like top round, top loin, or top sirloin. Serve with baked sweet potato and/or steamed broccoli (for tips on perfectly steaming broccoli, see page 157).   Yield: 4 servings

2 (8-ounce) sirloin tip-side steaks, trimmed of fat (about ¾ to 1 inch thick each)

1 tablespoon kosher salt

1 teaspoon ground black pepper

2 teaspoons fennel seeds

1 tablespoon garlic powder

1 teaspoon onion powder

1 tablespoon ground cumin

2 teaspoons ground coriander

1 teaspoon paprika

⅛ teaspoon ground cayenne pepper

⅛ teaspoon ground cloves

¼ cup extra-virgin olive oil, divided

Thirty minutes before serving time, remove the steak from the refrigerator and allow to reach room temperature. This will help ensure even heat distribution while cooking. While the steak is resting, place all remaining ingredients except the olive oil into a bowl and mix until well-combined. Then sprinkle the spice mixture across a large clean plate and set aside.

Pour 2 tablespoons of the olive oil into a large plastic zip-top bag. Using tongs, place one of the steaks into the bag, massaging the oil into the steak from the outside of the bag. Transfer the steak onto the plate to absorb the spices and then flip it over to season the other side. Next, place it onto its side, gently pressing it into the remaining spices on the plate, and then rotating it around until all sides have been thoroughly spiced. Be sure that every nook and cranny is covered with spice rub. Repeat this procedure with the second steak. As you finish spicing each steak, place them onto a clean plate and set aside.

In a sauté pan that closely fits the size of your steak, heat the remaining olive oil on high heat until glistening. Then add the first steak. When the steak makes contact with the pan, it should sizzle. If not, your pan's not hot enough. Cook for 3 to 4 minutes per side for medium rare and 4 to 5 minutes for medium. At about the halfway point, cut into the steak with a fork and knife to check for doneness, then flip to the other side when ready. Transfer the steak to a clean, heatproof plate, and let rest for at least 5 minutes before serving. Repeat the procedure with the second steak. Divide each steak into 2 portions and place onto dinner plates. Serve immediately.

Chef's Notes: Remember that once it's done, the steak's temperature will continue to rise a few more degrees as it rests, so be sure not to overcook your steak.

Teriyaki Hamburgers
with Wasabi-Avocado Sauce

This Japanese-inspired preparation is a novel and refreshing way to make hamburgers.   Yield: 4 patties

SAUCE

1 ripe medium-sized Haas avocado, peeled, pitted, and diced

½ teaspoon wasabi paste

1 tablespoon freshly squeezed lime juice (about ½ lime)

½ tablespoon sesame oil

½ tablespoon soy sauce

2 tablespoons scallions (about 1 scallion)

1 tablespoon fresh cilantro leaves

BURGER

2 pounds ground beef

½ teaspoon kosher salt

½ teaspoon coarsely ground black pepper

1 teaspoon garlic powder

1 teaspoon onion powder

½ teaspoon ground ginger

1 tablespoon white (or brown) sesame seeds

1 tablespoon teriyaki sauce (or if unavailable, soy sauce will work)

ASSEMBLY

sesame oil, for the grill

4 whole wheat burger buns

lettuce

4 large tomato slices

4 red onion ring slices (grilled or raw)

MAKE THE SAUCE: Combine all the sauce ingredients in a food processor and pulse until smooth. Transfer to a small dish and set aside.

MAKE THE BURGERS: Add all the burger ingredients to a medium, nonporous bowl, and then mix together with your hands until thoroughly combined. Form into two ½-inch-thick patties, place on a plate, and tightly cover with plastic wrap. Refrigerate, covered, for at least 30 minutes to let the flavors meld.

GRILL AND ASSEMBLE THE BURGERS: Lightly spray or brush a grill grate with sesame oil to prevent the patties from sticking. Then heat the grill to medium-high. Place patties on the hot grill, and cook for 3 to 5 minutes per side (for medium-rare), or until desired level of doneness has been reached. Remove from the grill and place onto buns. Add desired toppings and sauce, and serve.

Tequila-Lime Steak Fajitas

Tangy and flavorful, this version of steak fajitas is one that you won't forget anytime soon. This dish is sometimes served with Refried Beans (page 115) and Mexican rice, although I've found the fajitas by themselves to be more than enough food for a single meal. Yield: 4 to 6 servings

MARINADE

1 pound flank or skirt steak

1 teaspoon garlic powder

½ tablespoon mild Mexican chili powder

2 tablespoons paprika

½ tablespoon dried oregano

¼ teaspoon salt

1 teaspoon grated lime zest (from 1 large lime)

3 tablespoons freshly squeezed lime juice (from 1 large lime)

¼ cup gold tequila

FAJITAS

1 tablespoon extra-virgin olive oil

1 cup sliced yellow onion, cut into ½-inch-thick crescent slivers (about ½ medium onion)

1 to 2 tablespoons seeded, diced jalapeño pepper

1 cup sliced green bell pepper, cut into ½-inch-thick strips (about ½ large pepper)

1 cup sliced red bell pepper, cut into ½-inch-thick strips (about ½ large pepper)

¼ cup gold tequila

ACCOMPANIMENTS

4 to 6 medium, soft flour tortillas

prepared pico de gallo or other salsa

4 to 6 tablespoons shredded Monterey Jack cheese

4 to 6 tablespoons Greek yogurt

a few avocado slices or guacamole

2 tablespoons finely minced fresh cilantro, for garnish

MAKE THE MARINADE: Place the steak on an even, nonporous surface, cut on the bias into 1 x 3-inch thick strips, and transfer to a large plastic zip-top bag. Add the remaining marinade ingredients to the bag, seal, and refrigerate overnight or for at least 6 to 8 hours.

PREPARE THE FAJITAS: In a large pan or wok that's designed to withstand high heat, warm the olive oil over high heat. Reduce the heat to medium and sauté the onions until translucent, about 3 minutes. Then add the jalapeños and green and red bell peppers, and cook for about 2 more minutes, or until the onions turn golden brown and the peppers become tender. Deglaze with the tequila, stirring to loosen the fond (brown bits on the bottom of the pan), and cook for another 2 to 3 minutes, until the liquid reduces to a thin layer on the bottom of the pan. Remove from the heat, transfer to a medium bowl, and set aside. Turn up the heat to high, and sauté the steak in the residual olive oil and marinade juices for about 3 minutes per side (for medium-rare), or until cooked to desired level of doneness. (The steak will cook very quickly, as the pan should be very hot at this point. The steak should sizzle as soon as it hits the pan. If not, it's not hot enough. So make sure you watch the steak very carefully!) Transfer to a separate bowl and set aside.

ASSEMBLE THE FAJITAS: Divide the steak into equal portions. Place a small amount of steak onto each tortilla, then add the onions, peppers, and any toppings you'd like, such a pico de gallo, shredded cheese, a dollop of nonfat Greek yogurt, avocado slices or guacamole, and fresh cilantro.

> ## POWER TIP: AVOCADOS AND CAROTENOIDS
>
> Here's another major health benefit you'll get from avocados: Avocado oil boosts the absorption of beta-carotene and lycopene, two very important carotenoids (one of the major classes of phytonutrients) containing high levels of anti-oxidants, both of which are not-so-coincidentally found in copious amounts in the recipe for Baked Egg in an Avocado with Pico de Gallo (page 44). For example, tomatoes, are rich in both lycopene and beta-carotene.

Spaghetti Squash & Spicy Meatballs

This dish is great for post-exercise recovery or as a pre-race meal. For starters, spaghetti squash is an excellent source of nutritious, fiber-packed carbs and thus makes for an excellent pasta substitute. The combination of turkey and lean beef in the meatballs not only provides quality, muscle-building protein, but it also keeps the dish lean, nutritious, and flavorful. Notably, turkey is packed with all three essential branched chain amino acids (BCAAs), the building blocks of protein that play an essential role in energy production both during and after exercise. BCAAs are a key component of an athlete's dietary plan because they help improve exercise performance and reduce muscle protein breakdown. Our bodies don't produce BCAAs, so we need to get them from the foods we eat. Yield: 4 servings

3 pounds spaghetti squash, halved crosswise with a sharp chef's knife (about 1 medium-sized squash)

TOMATO SAUCE   Yield: 32 ounces

1 cup diced yellow onion

2 tablespoons finely minced garlic (about 4 large cloves)

4 cups vine-ripened tomatoes, diced (about 3 large tomatoes)

2 cups water (or more if necessary)

¼ cup tomato paste

¼ teaspoon salt

¼ teaspoon ground black pepper

¼ cup minced fresh basil, tightly packed, plus more for garnish

1 tablespoon coarsely chopped fresh oregano, tightly packed

1 tablespoon finely minced fresh marjoram, tightly packed

2 tablespoons finely minced fresh flat-leaf parsley, tightly packed

MEATBALLS

½ pound lean ground turkey

½ pound lean ground beef

¼ cup finely minced fresh spinach, tightly packed

2 eggs

¼ teaspoon ground black pepper

¼ teaspoon salt

½ teaspoon dried basil

2 tablespoons fresh flat-leaf parsley, finely minced and densely packed

½ teaspoon dried oregano

½ teaspoon garlic powder

½ teaspoon onion powder

2 teaspoons paprika

¼ teaspoon ground cayenne pepper

Preheat the oven to 375°F. Bring a large pot of water to a rolling boil, and then carefully place the squash halves into the pot using a sturdy pair of tongs. Boil for 20 to 25 minutes, or until tender. Let the squash cool for at least 10 minutes before handling. Then, using a large spoon, scoop out the pulp and seeds and discard. Separate the spaghetti squash strands with a fork, scraping with the grain of the noodles (crosswise). Use the same spoon you just used to scrape out all of the strands to remove the spaghetti squash strands en masse. Once you've loosened some of the strands, it'll be easier to insert your spoon closer to the rind and excavate the remainder. If you've cooked the squash for long enough, this should be relatively easy to do. Divide up the squash into 4 portions and place into bowls.

MAKE THE TOMATO SAUCE: Combine the onions, garlic, tomatoes, and water in a medium pot and bring to a boil, then reduce the heat and simmer for 15 minutes, stirring frequently. (If the mixture cooks down too quickly, reduce the heat a bit and/or add more water as necessary.) Add the tomato paste, season with salt and pepper, and then stir to break up the paste and fully incorporate. Add the basil, oregano, marjoram, and parsley, and continue to cook for another 5 minutes. Remove from the heat and set aside.

MAKE THE MEATBALLS: Place all of the meatball ingredients into a large bowl and thoroughly mix together using a spatula or fork. Using a cookie dough scoop (or small ice cream scoop), form bite-size meatballs and place as many as will fit into a large ovenproof skillet, cooking them in multiple batches until all the meatballs have been cooked. (No extra oil is needed as the rendered fat from the meat will be adequate to brown the meatballs and keep them from burning. If needed, you can always add a bit of water during cooking.) Place the meatballs into the oven and bake for 15 minutes total, or until golden brown. Then transfer the skillet from the oven to the stovetop, and sear on high heat for an additional 5 minutes, browning the meatballs on all sides. Remove from the heat, drain fat, and let cool for several minutes. Using a slotted spoon, divide the meatballs into equal portions and place on top of each bowl of squash. If needed, reheat the sauce, then pour it over the meatballs and squash. Garnish with additional basil, if desired.

Chef's Notes: If you like a smoother tomato sauce, you can always purée it in the blender first before pouring it over the meatballs. If you do this, be sure to let the sauce cool first before adding it to the blender so you avoid getting attacked by hot spurts of sauce.

Red Lentil & Garbanzo Bean Chili

Not only is vegan chili super easy to make, but it's great for fall and winter holiday parties (especially when served with baked tortilla chips!) and in cold weather, it really hits the spot. Plus, you don't have to be a vegetarian to enjoy vegetarian chili, so that means that this dish can be enjoyed by a wide array of people. An empty chili bowl at a party is always a good sign. Any leftovers you have will taste even better the next day, or even several days after that. It also freezes well, so if you're not in the mood to cook, all you have to do is wave your magic wand, and "poof!" an instant meal will "magically appear" on the table. Yield: 7 cups

1 cup red lentils, rinsed and picked over for stones and other debris

2 cups boiling hot water

1 tablespoon extra-virgin olive oil

1 cup diced yellow onion (1 small onion)

2 tablespoons finely minced garlic (about 4 large cloves)

1 large bay leaf

1 cup diced red bell pepper (about ¾ large pepper)

2 cups diced fresh vine-ripened tomatoes (about 3 large tomatoes)

1 (28-ounce) can crushed tomatoes

2 cups water or low-sodium vegetable broth

1 tablespoon apple cider vinegar

1 (15.5-ounce) can garbanzo beans, drained and rinsed

1 (6-ounce) can tomato paste

2 tablespoons Dutch-processed cocoa powder

1 tablespoon paprika

1 tablespoon ground coriander

1 tablespoon ground cumin

1 tablespoon mild Mexican-style chili powder

½ tablespoon ground cinnamon

½ teaspoon ground oregano

⅛ teaspoon ground cloves

⅛ teaspoon ground allspice

½ teaspoon salt

¼ teaspoon black pepper, or to taste (optional)

¼ cup masa harina (corn flour)

¼ cup chopped fresh cilantro, plus more for garnish

In advance, soak the lentils in the 2 cups boiling hot water for 1 hour, or until softened. (You can do this while you're prepping the vegetables.) Then, rinse and drain the lentils in a colander and set aside.

In a large pot, heat the olive oil on high until glistening. Then reduce the heat to low, add the onion, garlic, bay leaf, and red pepper, and sauté for about 5 minutes, or until tender. Add the diced fresh tomatoes followed by the canned, crushed tomatoes and cook for about 1 minute. Stir in the lentils and all of the remaining ingredients, except the masa harina and cilantro, cover with a lid, and simmer for 10 minutes. Then stir and check the liquid levels to make sure the chili isn't sticking to the bottom or burning. Add the 2 cups water or broth, or as needed. Cover again and cook for another 5 minutes. Stir in the masa harina. Cook, uncovered for 5 more minutes or until the lentils are soft, then let the chili cool for 5 to 10 minutes. Discard the bay leaf. Stir in the cilantro until evenly distributed. If desired, garnish with additional fresh cilantro and serve.

Bulgur, Black Bean, and Feta Stuffed Peppers

This recipe is a fusion of two different cuisines. Think of it as "Mexico, by way of Greece." There are all of the usual Mexican flavors and ingredients—cumin, fresh oregano, lime juice, jalapeño peppers, cilantro, and black beans—along with some complementary ingredients that are decidedly Greek, like feta, eggplant, tomatoes, and fresh mint. The nice thing about bulgur is that unlike other grains, it doesn't need to be cooked first, just soaked. This reduces this recipe's total prep time, which is ideal for busy athletes.   Yield: 4 servings

½ cup uncooked bulgur

2 cups water, for soaking

1 tablespoon extra-virgin olive oil

1 large bay leaf

¼ cup finely minced shallots

1 tablespoon finely minced garlic (about 2 large cloves)

2 cups unpeeled finely diced eggplant (in ½-inch cubes) (about ½ large eggplant)

¾ cup water or low-sodium vegetable broth, if preferred

3 tablespoons minced jalapeño pepper with seeds, stem, and ribs removed (about 1 large jalapeño pepper)

1 tablespoon finely minced fresh oregano, tightly packed

1 (15.5-ounce) can black beans, drained and rinsed

½ cup crumbled feta cheese

1 tablespoon ground cumin

1 tablespoon paprika

1 teaspoon ground coriander

⅜ teaspoon ground chipotle pepper

⅛ teaspoon salt, or to taste

⅛ teaspoon ground black pepper, or to taste

1 cup finely diced tomatoes (in ½-inch cubes) (about 1½ medium tomatoes)

2 tablespoons freshly squeezed lime juice

¼ cup finely minced fresh cilantro, tightly packed

2 tablespoons finely minced fresh mint, tightly packed

4 large, wide red or green bell peppers

Soak the bulgur in the 2 cups of water overnight. Then drain in a colander and squeeze to remove excess water. This should make 1 cup soaked bulgur.

In a large pot, heat the olive oil on high heat until glistening. Then reduce the heat to low, add the bay leaf, shallots, and garlic, and sauté for 5 minutes, or until tender. Next, stir in the diced eggplant, followed by ¾ cups water or vegetable stock. Turn up the heat to medium-high, cover with a lid, and cook for another 5 minutes. Reduce the heat to low. Stir in the jalapeño, fresh oregano, soaked bulgur, black beans, and feta. Season with the cumin, paprika, coriander, chipotle pepper, salt, and black pepper and cook, uncovered, for an additional 5 minutes, stirring frequently. Discard the bay leaf and remove from the heat. Allow to cool for 5 minutes, then stir in the diced tomatoes, lime juice, cilantro, and mint until well combined. Set aside.

Preheat the oven to 350°F. Slice the tops off the bell peppers and reserve. Remove the seeds and ribs from the peppers and place the bell pepper "cups" upright on an aluminum foil–lined 9 x 13-inch baking sheet and, using a large serving spoon, completely stuff each pepper (to the brim or slightly over) with an equal amount of the bulgur-vegetable filling (about 1 cup per pepper), making sure to compact each spoonful before adding another. Cover each pepper with its reserved top, followed by a small piece of foil. Mold foil around the sides of each pepper to secure. Place in the oven and cook for 50 to 60 minutes, or until the peppers are tender and juicy but still slightly firm and the filling is evenly heated throughout. (The filling should be hot but not intensely so.) About halfway through, lift up the foil and pepper tops to take a peek and check on their progress. Allow to cool for several minutes, then transfer to plates, and serve.

Chef's Notes: When selecting peppers for this recipe, be sure to pick large, squat, wide peppers that look like they can hold at least a cup of filling. The tall, skinny ones are a bit trickier to keep upright and their dimensions also make them harder to eat.

Red Beans & Black Rice

This Creole classic and Mardi Gras favorite makes an excellent pre-race or post-exercise recovery meal. Beans and rice are a great source of complex carbs, protein, and fiber, and thus have a lot of staying power. This version is fairly straightforward and traditional, except that it uses the superfood black rice (aka Chinese "forbidden rice," known for its antioxidant properties) instead of white and canned red beans versus dried ones, in order to expedite the cooking process, which is ideal for busy athletes. For authenticity, use Crystal brand hot sauce, which Louisianans swear by. Laissez les bon temps rouler! Yield: 3 to 4 servings

CREOLE SPICE MIX

1 tablespoon paprika

1 teaspoon garlic powder

1 teaspoon onion powder

½ teaspoon dried oregano

½ teaspoon dried thyme

⅜ teaspoon salt, or to taste

⅛ teaspoon ground black pepper

⅛ teaspoon ground cayenne pepper (or ground chipotle pepper, if you prefer a smoky flavor)

BEANS AND RICE

1 tablespoon extra-virgin olive oil

1 cup uncooked black rice

1 cup diced yellow onion (about ½ medium onion)

1 tablespoon finely minced garlic (about 2 large cloves)

½ cup finely chopped celery (about 2 celery ribs)

1 large bay leaf

4 cups water

1 (15.5-ounce) can kidney beans, drained and rinsed

½ cup finely diced green bell pepper (about ¼ large pepper)

¼ teaspoon (or more) cayenne pepper hot sauce (optional)

2 tablespoons fresh flat-leaf parsley, coarsely chopped

MAKE THE CREOLE SPICE MIX: Combine all the spice mix ingredients in a small bowl until well blended. Set aside.

MAKE THE BEANS AND RICE: Heat the olive oil over high heat in a large stockpot until glistening. Reduce the heat to low, then add the uncooked rice and brown for 2 minutes, stirring frequently to make sure the rice is completely coated with the olive oil. Let the rice crisp, but do not burn; crisping seals the rice's exterior to keep it from getting mushy when the water is added. Then add onions, garlic, celery, and bay leaf, and sauté for another 2 to 3 minutes, until tender. Add the water (it should sizzle when it hits the pan), then stir in the kidney beans, green bell peppers, hot sauce (if using), and reserved Creole spice mix. Stir to combine thoroughly. Turn up the heat to high and bring to a rolling boil, then reduce the heat to low again, quickly cover pot with a tightly fitting lid, and simmer for 40 minutes.

IMPORTANT: To perfectly cook the rice and maximize its fluffiness, do NOT, under any circumstances, lift the lid and peek at the rice while it's cooking. Only after the 40 minutes is up should you check the rice to see if it's ready. If necessary, use a glass lid so that you won't be tempted to peek.

When the rice is done, remove from the heat. At this point, the water should be fully absorbed and all of the rice grains should have split open. The rice should be fluffy, not dry or saucelike. If the grains are still hard and haven't yet split, add another 2 cups of water and cook for another 15 to 20 minutes or so. Allow the rice to steam, uncovered and undisturbed, for 5 to 10 minutes. Discard the bay leaf. Gently fluff with a fork. (For a more authentic consistency, you can mash the beans with a fork.) Garnish with parsley and serve hot.

Chef's Notes: Tabasco sauce or other hot pepper sauce can be substituted for the cayenne pepper sauce in a pinch.

Southwestern Black Bean Salsa Tortilla Wrap

This is a light and easy-to-make meal that's perfect for lunch. You can either eat one whole wrap that's been cut in half, or only eat one half with a soup or salad.   Yield: 6 to 8 wraps

BLACK BEAN SALSA

1 (15.5-ounce) can black beans, rinsed and drained

½ cup diced yellow bell pepper (about ½ medium pepper)

¼ cup diced red onion (about ¼ small onion)

1½ tablespoons stemmed, seeded, finely diced jalapeño (about ½ large pepper)

1 cup diced fresh, vine-ripened tomatoes (about 3 small tomatoes)

1 cup shredded Mexican four-cheese blend

½ cup sliced ripe California olives, drained

2 tablespoons scallions, green and white parts, sliced crosswise into ¼-inch rounds (about 1 large scallion)

2 teaspoons ground cumin

1 teaspoon dried oregano leaves

pinch of salt (optional)

⅛ teaspoon ground black pepper, or to taste

⅛ teaspoon ground chipotle pepper, or to taste

2 tablespoons finely minced fresh cilantro, tightly packed

2 tablespoons freshly squeezed lime juice (about 1 large lime)

1 cup diced Haas avocado (1 medium avocado)

½ cup frozen corn kernels, thawed and drained

OTHER INGREDIENTS

4 cups unsalted water, for cooking the corn, or as needed

4 to 6 extra-large (10-inch) low-fat flour tortillas

1 small romaine heart, leaves detached from base and washed well

MAKE THE SALSA: In a large bowl, thoroughly mix together all ingredients except for the avocado and corn. Then add avocado and gently combine. (Avocado tends to get mushy quickly if mixed too vigorously.) Make sure all the avocado is covered with lime juice, which will preserve it and keep it from oxidizing. Cover and refrigerate until serving time. (It's better to let the ingredients marinate a bit; this produces a tastier end result.)

STEAM THE CORN: Place a metal steamer basket into a large pot, and spread out its tabs so that it covers the entire bottom of the pot. Add roughly 4 cups of unsalted water to the pot, or however much water is needed to reach the base of the steamer. (Salted water toughens corn.) Bring the water to a rolling boil over high heat, about 8 minutes. Add the corn, cover the pot with its lid, and steam for 2 to 3 minutes, or until tender. Drain into a colander. Allow to cool for a few minutes. Add the steamed corn kernels to the salsa and gently mix.

ASSEMBLE THE WRAPS: Place each tortilla on a plate, then place half of a large romaine lettuce leaf (about a 4-inch piece) down the center of the tortilla. Next, place a line of black bean salsa down the center, about ¾ cup per wrap. (Don't overstuff the tortillas with filling or the wrap will be hard to close.) Fold over the bottom end (the end that's closest to you) of the tortilla, bringing it up only 2 to 3 inches toward the center. Then repeat for the opposite end. Starting from the sides of the tortilla that still remain open, roll the tortilla into a tight bundle. Grip the wrap firmly from one end while slicing into the center in a slightly diagonal direction. Repeat for each plate until all the wraps have been rolled. If you aren't serving them right away, wrap each one in aluminum foil or waxed paper and refrigerate until ready to serve.

Chef's Notes: You could also make the entire meal in advance and then take it to work for lunch. If you decide to do this, place the salsa in a plastic container with a lid and the tortilla and lettuce leaf into separate resealable plastic bags. Tortillas tend to dry out and harden when exposed to air for too long.

As a variation on a theme, substitute baby spinach or mixed spring greens (mesclun) for the romaine lettuce. Spinach tastes very mild and thus doesn't distract from the flavor of the wrap, while mixed spring greens will add a bit of peppery flavor. For added flavor and color, you could also use spinach- or tomato-flavored low-fat flour tortillas. Colorful wraps make for a presentation that's pleasing to the eye as well as the stomach.

Roasted Vegetable Pita Pizza

Pitas are the perfect size for making your own personal-sized pizzas. These colorful and easy-to-make pizzas are packed full of fiber, protein, and healthy carbs, which makes them deceptively filling. The vegetable toppings and freshly made pizza sauce, with its vine-ripened tomatoes and fresh herbs, are what give this recipe its vibrant flavors. Yield: 4 servings

TOMATO SAUCE

1 tablespoon olive oil

¼ cup finely minced shallot (about 1 large shallot)

1 tablespoon finely minced garlic (about 2 large cloves)

1 large bay leaf

½ cup water

1 (15-ounce) can crushed tomatoes

½ cup diced vine-ripened tomatoes

2 tablespoons tomato paste

1 teaspoon finely minced fresh oregano

¼ cup julienned fresh basil

2 teaspoons fresh thyme leaves

PIZZA

4 large (7½-inch) whole wheat pitas

1 cup shredded mozzarella cheese, divided

½ cup soft goat cheese (chèvre), crumbled

1 cup thinly sliced orange bell pepper (about ¾ large pepper)

½ cup Greek olives, pitted and sliced

2 tablespoons julienned fresh basil, divided

Preheat the oven to 400°F.

MAKE THE TOMATO SAUCE: In a medium saucepan, heat the olive oil on high until glistening. Then reduce the heat to low, add the shallots, garlic, and bay leaf, and sauté for 5 minutes, or until tender. Add the water, crushed canned tomatoes, vine-ripened tomatoes, and tomato paste, and stir until the tomato paste has been fully incorporated. Increase the heat to high, bring to a boil, then reduce the heat to medium-low. Add the oregano, basil, and thyme, and cook for an additional 5 minutes. Let cool, discard the bay leaf, and set aside.

MAKE THE PIZZA: Arrange the pitas on a metal baking sheet. Spread sauce onto each pizza with the back of a large spoon, then sprinkle with equal amounts of mozzarella cheese, followed by equal amounts of goat cheese, bell pepper, and olives. Bake for 8 to 10 minutes, or until the pizza has reached the desired level of crispness. Top with julienned basil and serve hot.

Chef's Notes: To save time, make the pizza sauce a few days in advance of when you plan to serve it. If stored in a tightly sealed container, the sauce will keep for several days in the refrigerator.

Cavatappi with Walnut-Almond Pesto & Sun-Dried Tomatoes

Cavatappi is a type of pasta in a corkscrew shape. To save time, buy precut sun-dried tomatoes and the kind that have been soaked in olive oil.   Yield: 4 servings

PASTA

6 quarts lightly salted water, seasoned with a few drops of olive oil

2 cups uncooked cavatappi pasta

1 cup julienned sun-dried tomatoes

½ cup (or more) julienned fresh basil leaves, tightly packed, plus more for garnish

2 tablespoons grated Parmesan cheese

PESTO   Yield: ¾ cup

1 cup fresh basil leaves and stems, tightly packed

2¼ teaspoons minced garlic (about 1½ large cloves)

¼ cup slivered almonds

¼ cup chopped walnuts

3 tablespoons extra-virgin olive oil

1 tablespoon freshly squeezed lemon juice

½ tablespoon light silken tofu

⅛ teaspoon salt

MAKE THE PASTA: About a half hour before serving time, bring the water to a rolling boil in a medium stockpot. Add the cavatappi and cook according to the package instructions.

MAKE THE PESTO: While you're waiting for the water to boil, place all the pesto ingredients into a food processor and pulse until well combined. Set aside.

When the pasta is ready, drain into a large colander, shock with cold running water, then drain again and pour back into the stockpot. Add the pesto and sun-dried tomatoes and stir until the pasta is well coated. Divide into equal portions and serve warm or at room temperature. Sprinkle each portion with Parmesan cheese and a small handful of julienned basil.

Chef's Notes: Pesto can be made in advance and refrigerated for up to 4 days or frozen for future use for about 6 to 8 months. Store it in a tightly sealed container or plastic freezer bag. For easier and faster defrosting, place individual-sized portions in ice cube trays and then place trays into tightly sealed freezer bags. Also, when you thaw the pesto, you might need to add more lemon juice, as the flavor of the lemon juice tends to fade with freezing.

Savory Noodle Kugel

Noodle kugel is a baked egg noodle and cheese casserole that Ashkenazi Jews brought over with them when they immigrated to America. This particular recipe is both light and satisfying, and, unlike most traditional noodle kugel recipes, is low in saturated fat. It's also got cottage cheese, which is packed with loads of isoleucine and leucine, two muscle-building essential branched chain amino acids (BCAAs). Yield: 8 to 10 servings

1 (12-ounce) bag wide egg noodles

½ tablespoon extra-virgin olive oil

2 cups (1 pound) nonfat small-curd cottage cheese

1½ cups nonfat plain Greek yogurt, divided

2 extralarge eggs

2 tablespoons very finely minced shallot (about 1 medium shallot)

1¼ teaspoons salt, or to taste

½ teaspoon ground black pepper, or to taste

2 tablespoons finely minced flat-leaf parsley, tightly packed (or 2 teaspoons dried parsley)

1 tablespoon finely minced fresh oregano, tightly packed (or 1 teaspoon dried oregano)

2 tablespoons finely minced fresh basil, tightly packed (or 2 teaspoons dried basil)

1 tablespoon fresh marjoram leaves, finely minced and tightly packed (or 1 teaspoon dried marjoram)

Preheat the oven to 375°F. Using a wide pastry brush, lightly coat a 9 x 13-inch glass baking dish with the olive oil.

In a large pot of boiling salted water, cook the noodles until tender, according to the package instructions. (Most wide egg noodles take no more than 7 to 9 minutes, maximum, to cook.) Drain and rinse them with cold water, then set aside.

In the bowl of a stand mixer fitted with the whisk attachment, whip the cottage cheese and 1 cup of the Greek yogurt on medium-high speed. Then add the eggs, shallots, salt, and black pepper, one ingredient at a time, and continue whipping until smooth, thick, and creamy. Turn off the mixer and fold in the parsley, oregano, basil, marjoram, and noodles, and spread the mixture evenly across the baking dish. Cover with aluminum foil and bake for 30 minutes, or until the kugel sets. Then remove the foil, and cook for an additional 10 to 15 minutes, or until the top turns a light golden brown. Open the oven, slide out the tray, and test the kugel for doneness by cutting into it with a knife. It should be somewhat solid and give some resistance when you cut through it. If it's too soft or there's still too much moisture, then bake it for an additional 15 to 20 minutes, or until further solidified. Allow it to cool for 10 minutes. Cut into 3-inch squares, top each portion with about 1 tablespoon of the remaining Greek yogurt, and serve.

Chef's Notes: If this is your first time making kugel and you'd prefer to try the traditional version instead as your first experience, just follow the same basic instructions above but omit the shallots, parsley, oregano, basil, and marjoram.

Zucchini "Fettuccine" Alfredo

Most people probably think "fattening" when the word "Alfredo" is mentioned, but below you'll find some cool tricks for making Alfredo sauce taste flavorful and creamy without all the heaviness and loads of saturated fat. And because this recipe combines the sauce with zucchini "noodles" instead of traditional semolina pasta, you'll actually be able to rise from the table without feeling like you're going to shift the earth's gravitational force and send it flying directly into the sun. Even better, there'll be no bloated feeling or starch-induced coma afterward. So, I hope you'll enjoy this recipe, content in the knowledge that you'll be feeding your family healthy, satisfying, and delicious food. Yield: 2 servings

4 long, medium zucchini, peeled and julienned lengthwise into long, thin "noodles" (about ¼ inch thick)

1 tablespoon extra-virgin olive oil

2 tablespoons finely minced garlic (about 4 large cloves)

½ cup finely minced shallot (about 2 large shallots)

2 cups low-fat buttermilk

1 tablespoon cornstarch or arrowroot powder

1⅓ cups grated Parmesan cheese

¼ teaspoon ground nutmeg

¼ teaspoon salt, or to taste

¼ teaspoon ground black pepper, or to taste

1 tablespoon fresh thyme, tightly packed

2 teaspoons finely minced fresh marjoram, tightly packed

½ cup unsweetened plain soy milk

1 tablespoon coarsely chopped flat-leaf parsley, coarsely chopped

Bring a pot of water to a rolling boil over high heat, then add the zucchini and cook for 6 to 8 minutes, or until tender but still firm. Drain, place in a large serving bowl, and set aside.

While the zucchini is cooking, make the sauce. In a separate pot, heat the olive oil on high heat until glistening. Then reduce the heat to low, add the garlic and shallots, and sauté for 5 minutes, or until tender. Next, add the buttermilk, followed by the cornstarch or arrowroot powder, stirring to fully combine. Add the Parmesan cheese, nutmeg, salt, and pepper and cook for 10 minutes, stirring constantly. Add the thyme, marjoram, and soy milk, and cook for an additional 5 minutes, continuing to stir. Remove from the heat and set aside. Allow to cool for 5 minutes, pour the sauce over the zucchini, and gently toss to combine. (Cooked zucchini is very delicate, so take special care not to demolish it while mixing in the sauce.) Garnish with parsley and serve.

Grilled "Polenta-Style" Quinoa Cakes
with Mushroom Ragù

This recipe is deceptively filling. Two cakes with ragù should be enough to feed a hungry athlete with a hearty appetite. If you're serving it as a side dish, plan on about one cake per person.   Yield: 8 (2½-inch) quinoa cakes

QUINOA CAKE

½ cup uncooked quinoa, thoroughly washed and drained

2 cups water

1 cup almond meal, plus more for dusting

1 cup grated Parmesan cheese

¼ cup crumbled soft goat cheese (chèvre)

1 teaspoon garlic powder

1 teaspoon onion powder

¼ teaspoon ground black pepper

⅛ teaspoon salt

1 tablespoon extra-virgin olive oil

RAGÙ

1 tablespoon extra-virgin olive oil

½ cup finely minced shallot (about 2 shallots)

1½ tablespoons finely minced garlic (about 3 large cloves)

1 cup sliced button mushrooms, in bite-size pieces

1 cup sliced portobello mushrooms, in bite-size pieces

1 cup sliced shiitake mushrooms, in bite-size pieces

¼ teaspoon salt

¼ teaspoon ground black pepper

1 tablespoon finely minced fresh rosemary

1 tablespoon finely minced fresh sage

¼ cup marsala wine (or sherry, if unavailable)

1 tablespoon fresh thyme

¼ cup low-fat unsweetened soy milk

1 tablespoon fresh flat-leaf parsley

MAKE THE QUINOA CAKES: Soak the quinoa for 10 to 15 minutes, then drain. Bring the water to a rolling boil in a large sauce pan. Add the quinoa and cook, covered, for 10 minutes. Allow to rest for 10 minutes to cool to room temperature, then fluff with a fork. Drain into a fine-mesh sieve and rinse with cold water. Transfer the cooled quinoa to a food processor followed by all the remaining quinoa cake ingredients, except the olive oil, which will be used later to sauté the cakes. Process until the quinoa is completely pulverized and all ingredients are fully incorporated.

Dust a large plate with a generous amount of almond meal. Then break off a large chunk of dough about the size of a golf ball (about 1¾ inch in diameter) and roll into a ball with the palms of your hand. With the palm of your hand, gently flatten the dough ball so that it's about ¼ inch high, then shape and smooth the outer edges into a seamless disc. Place the dough disc onto the almond meal "floured" plate; flip to flour on both sides. Repeat this process until all the dough has been used up and you've made 8 uniformly sized cakes. Set aside.

MAKE THE RAGÙ: Heat the olive oil over high heat until glistening. Then reduce the heat to low, add the shallots and garlic, and sauté for 2 minutes. Then add all of the mushrooms and immediately season with salt to help accelerate the moisture extraction process. Turn up the heat to medium. Quickly add the pepper, rosemary, and sage and cook for 10 minutes, or until the liquid has evaporated to a thin layer on the bottom of the pan, stirring occasionally. Stir in the marsala to deglaze, stirring to loosen the fond (the brown bits on the bottom of the pan). Cook another 5 minutes, or until the liquid has once again been reduced to a thin layer on the bottom of the pan. Add the thyme and soy milk and continue to cook until the liquid has been reduced by at least three-quarters, about 5 more minutes. In the final 1 to 2 minutes of cooking, add the parsley. Remove from the heat and set aside.

GRILL AND ASSEMBLE THE QUINOA CAKES: Heat the 1 tablespoon olive oil in a square grill pan over high heat until glistening, 20 to 30 seconds, then reduce the heat to medium-low, place 4 quinoa cakes into the pan, and cook about 3 minutes per side. Place onto a clean plate and set aside. Repeat with the remaining quinoa cakes. Divide the cakes into equal portions, transfer to plates, then top with ragù and serve.

Chef's Notes: It's important to thoroughly wash quinoa to remove the saponin, which creates a bitter taste. This makes a huge difference in flavor and palatability. I've heard people say that quinoa tastes bitter, but really, it's because whoever prepared it for them probably didn't wash it first.

Also, be sure to thoroughly clean the mushrooms to remove any debris. The best way to do this is to soak them in a bowl of cold water for 15 to 20 minutes, then rinse them under cold water, washing them by hand.

You can buy almond meal at many, if not most, generic grocery stores these days. (Or at least you can in major cities.) I know for a fact that Whole Foods and Trader Joe's carry almond meal. It's a fairly neutral tasting "flour," which makes it the perfect canvas and/or binding agent for many different dishes, including this one.

POWER TIP: QUINOA

Quinoa is so versatile and very healthy to boot. For starters, it's a complete protein, containing all nine amino acids. Quinoa has large amounts of lysine, an amino acid essential to tissue growth and repair. It's also an excellent source of magnesium, iron, copper, and phosphorus. Please be aware that it also contains a decent amount of tryptophan, so you might not want to eat it with turkey, unless you've cleared your schedule for a three-hour nap after mealtime. Quinoa is also supposed to be good for cardiovascular health and may also help those with migraine headaches, asthma, atherosclerosis, breast cancer, and/or diabetes.

Greek-Style Eggplant Gratin
with Feta & Tomato Sauce

Think of this recipe as the Greek version of eggplant Parmesan.   Yield: 6 servings

SAUCE

1 tablespoon extra-virgin olive oil

½ cup diced yellow onion

1 tablespoon finely minced garlic

2 cups diced vine-ripened tomatoes (about 3 medium tomatoes)

2 tablespoons tomato paste

½ tablespoon finely minced fresh rosemary leaves, tightly packed

1 tablespoon finely minced fresh oregano leaves, tightly packed

1 tablespoon finely minced fresh flat-leaf parsley, tightly packed

1 tablespoon finely minced fresh mint, tightly packed

⅛ teaspoon salt

⅛ teaspoon ground black pepper

GRATIN

1 cup shredded mozzarella cheese

1 cup crumbled feta cheese

½ large eggplant, sliced crosswise into 12 (¼-inch-thick) rounds

Preheat the oven to 375°F. Set a 9 x 11-inch glass baking dish on top of an 11 x 17-inch baking sheet. This will prevent liquids from bubbling over onto the oven's surfaces during baking.

MAKE THE SAUCE: Heat the olive oil over high heat in a large pot until glistening. Then reduce the heat to low, add the onions and garlic, and cook for 5 minutes, or until tender, stirring occasionally. Add the vine-ripened tomatoes, tomato paste, and rosemary, and cook for 5 minutes. Then stir in the oregano, parsley, mint, salt, and pepper, and cook for 5 minutes more. Remove from the heat and set aside, allowing sauce to cool slightly.

MAKE THE GRATIN: Combine the mozzarella and feta cheese in a bowl and mix thoroughly. Pour half of the sauce onto the bottom of the baking dish, using the back of a spoon to evenly distribute. Then place a layer of 6 eggplant slices on top. Sprinkle half of the mozzarella-feta mixture over the eggplant. Repeat this process with the second layer. Cover the dish with aluminum foil and bake for 45 minutes, then remove the foil and bake for 15 minutes more, or until the top is bubbly and golden brown. Serve immediately.

Thai Vegetable Stir-Fry

Serve this dish as a vegetarian or vegan entrée, or as a side dish.   Yield: 3 to 4 servings

4 pieces fresh lemongrass, vertically scored then cut crosswise into 3-inch pieces (about 1 stalk)

1 tablespoon sesame seed oil

1 inch fresh ginger, peeled and julienned into thin matchsticks (about 2 tablespoons)

½ cup diced yellow onion (about ½ small onion)

1 tablespoon finely minced garlic (about 2 large cloves)

2 cups sliced Chinese eggplant

4 to 6 small red Thai chilies, seeded, and diced

1¼ cup diced yellow bell peppers (about 1 large pepper)

2 cups diced oyster mushrooms (about 1 pound)

1½ cups light silken tofu, diced

⅛ teaspoon salt, or to taste

⅛ teaspoon ground black pepper, or to taste

¼ cup sliced scallions, white and green parts, in ¼-inch-thick rounds (about 2 large scallions)

¼ cup julienned fresh basil, tightly packed

1 tablespoon sesame seeds

Unfurl the scored lemongrass and set aside. Heat the sesame seed oil over medium heat in a large wok. Add the ginger, onions, garlic, and lemongrass, reduce the heat to low, and sauté for 5 minutes. Add the eggplant slices and cook until tender. Next, add the Thai chilies, bell pepper, mushrooms, and tofu, and cook for another 2 to 3 minutes, stirring occasionally. Season with salt and pepper, and then stir once more. In the last minute of cooking, add the scallions. When the vegetables are ready—they should be tender and maintain their color but still be slightly firm—remove from the heat. Divide into equal portions. Garnish with basil, sprinkle with sesame seeds, and serve.

Chef's Notes: If you can't find fresh lemongrass, substitute with one of the following: 2 (3-inch) pieces dried lemongrass soaked in hot water for 2 hours, 1 teaspoon lemongrass (sereh) powder, or the grated zest of 1 lemon.

Grilled Vegetable Panini with Buffalo Mozzarella

Mozzarella contains 32 percent protein, second highest in protein only to Parmesan and Romano cheeses.   Yield: 1 sandwich

2 tablespoons extra-virgin olive oil, divided (for coating the bottom of the pan)

1 tablespoon freshly squeezed lemon juice

¼ teaspoon kosher salt, or to taste

⅛ teaspoon ground black pepper, or to taste

½ teaspoon ground marjoram

1 teaspoon ground oregano

¼ pound eggplant, sliced crosswise in ¼-inch-thick rounds

½ cup sliced orange bell pepper, in long, ½-inch-thick strips (about ¼ large pepper)

1 cup thinly sliced oyster mushrooms

2 teaspoons finely minced garlic (about 1½ large cloves)

2 large, thick slices of rustic bread

¼ cup fresh mozzarella slices

6 large whole fresh basil leaves, for garnish

Place 1 tablespoon of the olive oil and the lemon juice, salt, pepper, marjoram, and oregano in a large zip-top bag. Add the eggplant, bell pepper, and mushrooms, and seal the bag. Thoroughly massage the ingredients from the outside of the bag to combine. Let marinate for about 30 minutes at room temperature.

With a pastry brush, evenly coat the bottom of a nonstick square grill pan with a thin layer of the olive oil (about ½ tablespoon). Make sure the oil gets into the grooves of the pan, which will ensure that the vegetables cook but don't get soaked in the oil. (This way, the olive oil will bubble up from the grooves on occasion, but won't saturate the vegetables.)

Set a stovetop range to medium-high heat and warm the grill pan. Grill the eggplant slices first for a few minutes before adding the other vegetables, since they'll take the longest to cook. Next, add the orange bell pepper, followed by the oyster mushrooms. Cook all of the vegetables for several minutes per side, until you get nice grill marks on both sides. When ready, transfer the vegetables to a small bowl and set aside.

Next, add the garlic in a small corner of the pan, and cook until the raw smell disappears. This should only take a few seconds, so watch the garlic carefully to make sure it doesn't burn. Turn off the heat and scoop out the garlic with a heatproof, nonmetal spatula to avoid scratching the pan. Add the garlic to the same bowl as the other vegetables and thoroughly combine. Set aside.

Brush the pan once more with 1 teaspoon of the olive oil. Turn the heat back to medium-high and grill the bread slices on one side until grill marks appear, flip, and then grill bread on the other side, quickly topping one of the face-up sides with mozzarella. Bread slices will cook very quickly, so check the undersides by lifting them up with a spatula after about a minute or so. When ready, remove from the heat and transfer to a plate.

On one of the bread slices, pile on vegetables, evenly distributing them in layers across the bread. Top the final layer with whole, fresh basil leaves, and close the sandwich by placing the other slice on top, cheese side facedown. Serve immediately.

Cold Sesame Noodles

Looking for a filling yet nutritious meal? This dish is your ticket. It's got quality protein and carbs, along with some healthy fats, not to mention it's satisfying to both the taste buds and stomach. Yield: 2 servings

NOODLES

4 ounces soba (buckwheat) noodles

6 to 8 cups water

½ cup julienned carrots (about 1 medium carrot)

½ cup julienned seedless cucumber (about ½ large cucumber)

2 tablespoons chopped scallions, white and green parts

2 tablespoons coarsely chopped fresh cilantro, tightly packed

PEANUT SAUCE

½ cup creamy-style peanut butter

½ tablespoon minced garlic (about 4 medium cloves)

½ tablespoon minced fresh ginger (about a 1-inch piece)

½ teaspoon salt, or to taste

pinch of red chile pepper flakes

1 tablespoon finely minced fresh cilantro, tightly packed

½ tablespoon freshly squeezed lime juice

1 tablespoon soy sauce

2 tablespoons honey

1 tablespoon sesame seed oil

¼ cup canned light coconut milk

2 tablespoons water (or more, as needed)

½ tablespoon sesame seeds

In a medium stockpot, boil soba noodles (on high) for 4 minutes until al dente. Pour the noodles into a colander over the sink, rinse with cold water, and drain. Pour into a large bowl and set aside. Wash out the pot. Put all peanut sauce ingredients into a food processor and pulse until smooth. (This step can be done in advance to reduce meal prep time.) Cook for 3 to 4 minutes on medium-low heat in the same pot you used for the noodles, or until the raw garlic smell disappears, stirring continually. (Add more water as necessary to prevent burning the bottom of the sauce and achieve desired consistency.) Gently fold in the sesame seeds and then pour the sauce into a bowl with noodles. Add the carrots, cucumbers, scallions, and cilantro, and toss until all the noodles have been evenly coated with sauce.

Mushroom-Olive Quinoa Pilaf with Fresh Herbs

This delicious high-protein dish can be served as a main course or side.   Yield: 2 servings

1 cup uncooked quinoa, rinsed

1 tablespoon extra-virgin olive oil

1 tablespoon finely minced garlic (about 2 large cloves)

1 cup thinly sliced common mushrooms (about 3 large mushrooms)

¼ teaspoon salt

¼ teaspoon ground black pepper

¼ cup dry white wine

2½ cups water

1 teaspoon julienned fresh rosemary, tightly packed

½ teaspoon julienned fresh sage, densely packed

16 large kalamata olives, pitted and sliced crosswise into ¼-inch-thick rounds (about ½ cup)

¼ cup finely minced fresh flat-leaf parsley, tightly packed

¼ cup fresh basil leaves, julienned and tightly packed

½ cup grated Parmigiano-Reggiano cheese *

Soak the quinoa in water for 15 minutes, then drain and set aside. In a medium sauce pan, heat the olive oil over high heat until glistening. Then reduce the heat to low, add the garlic, and sauté for 2 to 3 minutes. Do not let the garlic brown. Next add the mushrooms, season with salt and pepper, and gently stir to combine. Cook for another minute, then add the quinoa. Stir ingredients until just combined, and cook for 1 minute more, allowing the quinoa to crisp slightly. Immediately add the white wine to deglaze, stirring to loosen the fond (the brown bits on the bottom of the pan) and cook until the liquid has been reduced to a thin layer on the bottom of the pan, about 5 minutes. Pour in the water, stir to combine, then cover with a clear glass lid, and bring to a rolling boil. Then reduce the heat to low again and simmer for 10 to 15 minutes, or until the water has been completely absorbed.

With about 5 minutes of cooking time left, add the rosemary and sage, followed by the kalamata olives. During the final minute of cooking, lift the lid, and taste for consistency; if the quinoa is still a bit too hard and crunchy, then add more water as needed, 1 cup at a time, waiting until each cup has been absorbed before adding the next, and continue to cook until the grains soften to the desired consistency. Be careful not to overcook. You don't want it to be mushy; it should still have a slight crunch to it when it's done cooking, but it shouldn't be so hard that it'll break your teeth. When ready, remove from the heat, open the lid, add the parsley, basil, and cheese, and stir until just combined. Cover once again and let stand for 10 to 15 minutes, then uncover and gently fluff once. Serve immediately.

Chef's Notes: To make this recipe vegan, omit the Parmigiano-Reggiano cheese, or replace with a non-dairy cheese substitute.

Chana Masala

Chana masala, also sometimes referred to as chole masala, is a savory, tangy chickpea and tomato dish commonly found on most Northern Indian and Pakistani restaurant menus. It's particularly popular in the Northwest Indian states of Punjab, Gujarat, and Rajasthan. Chana masala has a somewhat sour, lemony flavor, due to the addition of dried mango powder, or amchur (sometimes spelled amchoor) in Hindi. In general, traditional Indian cooking often calls for cream, and often lots of it, and the standard, much denser rendition of the sauce in this dish is no different. Instead, this recipe uses coconut milk, which essentially achieves the same effect as the cream in terms of flavor, texture, and overall consistency; it brings the same richness and depth of flavor, but without any of the accompanying health issues that go along with the consumption of animal-based saturated fats. Not only is the coconut milk a lot healthier, but it also complements the chana perfectly. Its flavor blends seamlessly with the other ingredients and it just makes this dish taste divine! Serve with Aromatic Basmati Rice (page 126) and/or naan. Yield: About 6 cups, or 6 to 8 servings*

1 tablespoon extra-virgin coconut oil

2 cups Vidalia (or yellow) onion, peeled and diced (about 1 medium onion)

2 tablespoons fresh ginger, peeled and julienned into 1-inch-long matchsticks

1 tablespoon finely minced garlic (about 2 large cloves)

2 (15.5-ounce) cans chickpeas

1 (28-ounce) can crushed tomatoes

3 tablespoons tomato paste

½ cup light coconut milk

2 tablespoons Garam Masala (page 63)

½ tablespoon amchur, or to taste (see note)

¼ teaspoon ground turmeric

1½ cups diced vine-ripened tomatoes (about 2½ small tomatoes)

¼ teaspoon salt, or to taste

½ cup coarsely chopped fresh cilantro

raita, to serve (optional)

Heat the coconut oil in a large (12 to 13-inch) sauté pan over medium heat until glistening. Reduce the heat to low and add the diced onions and ginger matchsticks and sauté until tender, about 3 minutes. Add the garlic and cook an additional 2 minutes. Next, add the chickpeas, crushed tomatoes, tomato paste, and coconut milk, and stir until well combined. Stir in the garam masala, amchur, and turmeric, and reduce the liquid in the pan by ¼ of its original volume. Be sure to stir continually so that the sauce doesn't burn or stick to the bottom of the pan. Next, add the vine-ripened tomatoes, season with salt, and continue to cook just until the tomatoes soften a bit. Be careful not to overcook the tomatoes; they should still maintain their form and color, and still have a slight crunch to them when you've finished cooking. (If the mixture cooks down too quickly, add water as necessary, ¼ cup at a time.) When finished, remove from the heat, mix in the cilantro, and divide into equal portions. Top with raita if so desired.

Chef's Notes: If you are going to serve the chana masala with rice, then I'd recommend making the rice while the chana is cooking, to save time.

If you can't find amchur locally (in an Indian grocery store), then you can always order it online. Alternatively, you can substitute it in this recipe with 1 tablespoon freshly squeezed lemon juice. If using lemon juice for the amchur, then be sure to add it towards the end. Lemon juice's chemical composition becomes altered with heat, and will thus affect the other ingredients it comes into contact with them in the pan.

Side Dishes

Parmesan-Crusted Asparagus in White Truffle Oil

Power your workouts with these deliciously crispy Parmesan-covered asparagus spears! Yield: 4 to 6 servings

1 pound green asparagus spears, trimmed of tough, woody ends

2 tablespoons white truffle oil

1 tablespoon freshly squeezed lemon juice

½ teaspoon garlic powder

¼ teaspoon salt

⅛ teaspoon ground black pepper

⅛ teaspoon red chile pepper flakes

½ cup grated Parmesan cheese

Preheat the oven to 400°F. Lay the asparagus spears on an 11 x 17-inch aluminum foil–covered baking sheet and drizzle with the white truffle oil and lemon juice. Lightly sprinkle with garlic powder, salt, black pepper, and red chile pepper flakes from a good vertical distance for even distribution. Bake in the oven for 6 to 8 minutes per side, or until tender. Then open the oven, sprinkle with cheese, and bake for 1 to 2 minutes more, or until the cheese begins to bubble and turn golden brown.

POWER TIP: ASPARAGUS

Asparagus has a multitude of benefits for athletic performance: It's anti-inflamatory and antioxidative; boosts energy levels (by accelerating the body's metabolization of carbohydrates, fats, and proteins into energy); supports cardiovascular, bone, and digestive tract health; accelerates tissue repair (useful for post-exercise muscle tissue repair); and provides a decent amount of electrolytes (potassium) and even a small amount of muscle-building protein and glycogen-replenishing carbs. Asparagus also helps to regulate blood sugar and blood fat levels, supports digestive tract health, and fights cancer, heart disease, and type-2 diabetes.

Refried Beans

This supereasy and quick dish goes well with so many different Mexican foods: It makes a great side for steak or chicken fajitas, Vegetable Quesadillas (page 57), pupusas, empanadas, or Huevos Rancheros (page 46). It can also be served alongside Mexican rice.   Yield: 4 servings

1 tablespoon extra-virgin olive oil

⅔ cup finely minced yellow onion (about ½ large onion)

1 teaspoon garlic, peeled and finely minced (about ½ large clove)

1 (15.5-ounce) can pinto beans, drained and rinsed, then mashed with a fork or potato masher

¼ cup water, or more as needed

⅛ teaspoon salt, or to taste

¼ teaspoon ground cumin

¼ teaspoon ground coriander

¼ teaspoon dried oregano

Heat the olive oil in a large sauté pan over high heat. Then reduce the heat to low, add the onions, and sauté until translucent, about 5 minutes. After about 4 minutes, add the garlic so that it's softened but not browned. Turn up the heat to medium-low and add the mashed pinto beans and ¼ cup water. Add the salt, cumin, coriander, and oregano, stir thoroughly, and cook for 2 to 3 more minutes, or until heated through. If necessary, add more water to the pan during cooking if the existing liquid starts to evaporate too quickly. Remove from the heat and transfer to a serving dish or divide into equal portions and serve.

Oven-Baked Rosemary-Parmesan Sweet Potato Fries

With all of the benefits from the beta-carotene and vitamin A in sweet potatoes, who can resist the lure of these flavorful, crunchy fries? Yield: 1 to 2 servings

6 ounces sweet potato, scrubbed and unpeeled (about 1 medium sweet potato)

¼ cup extra-virgin olive oil

¼ cup grated Parmesan cheese

2 tablespoons finely minced fresh rosemary, tightly packed

1 tablespoon paprika

1 tablespoon cornstarch

¼ teaspoon kosher salt, or to taste

¼ teaspoon ground black pepper, or to taste

½ teaspoon garlic powder

½ teaspoon onion powder

Preheat the oven to 450°F and cover an 11 x 17-inch baking sheet with aluminum foil (for easy cleanup). Uniformly slice the sweet potato into quarters, then again lengthwise into ¼-inch-thick slices, with the peel side facing up. Then lay each slice flat and cut into long, ⅜-inch-thick strips. Put the strips into a large shallow bowl and pour in the olive oil. Thoroughly combine all the remaining ingredients in a small bowl, then sprinkle over sweet potatoes.

Wearing latex or rubber gloves to keep your hands clean and oil-free, toss all of the ingredients together with your hands until the sweet potatoes are thoroughly and evenly coated with oil, rosemary leaves, cheese, and spices. Using tongs, shake off the excess oil into the bowl and transfer the sweet potatoes to the prepared baking sheet, arranging them in a single layer spaced evenly apart. Bake on the top shelf of the oven for 18 to 20 minutes, or until golden brown. Allow to cool for a few minutes. Then use tongs to transfer to a large, paper towel–covered tray to drain the excess oil. (You can also pat them with another paper towel to blot more oil.) Divide into equal portions and serve immediately.

POWER TIP: SWEET POTATOES

As a high-satiety food that's packed with nutrients, sweet potatoes have some amazing health benefits that are of particular use to athletes. For starters, they have very strong anti-inflammatory properties, which helps reduce post-exercise inflammation. Olive oil, another ingredient in this recipe, has anti-inflammatory phytonutrients as well. Additionally, both olive oil and sweet potatoes are rich in antioxidants, which help counter the effects of free-radical damage that occurs during exercise, particularly during aerobic activity. The antioxidants in phytonutrients have also been shown to reduce post-exercise muscle soreness and may also enhance muscle repair. Particularly effective in this regard are vitamins A and E, which are found in sweet potatoes and olive oil, respectively. In fact, sweet potatoes contain copious amounts of vitamin A, at 38,433 IU per cup, which is 769% of the recommended daily allowance (RDA)!

Tabouleh

As this recipe shows, parsley isn't just for decoration. This often underappreciated herb is also very nutritious as well. Several other ingredients in tabouleh are also extremely healthy for you. For example, the whole grain bulgur is not just a great source of fiber but also contains several important vitamins, minerals, and hundreds of unique phytochemicals, which, as research suggests, may collectively work together to reduce one's risk of certain chronic diseases and gastrointestinal cancers. Yield: 8 to 10 servings as a small side, 4 to 6 as a main course

1 cup bulgur (medium grade)

2 cups cold water

3 cups finely minced flat-leaf parsley (about 2 large bunches)

1 cup finely minced fresh mint

1½ cups diced red onion (about 1 small onion)

1½ cups sliced scallions, white and green parts, (about 8 scallions)

2 cups diced cucumber (about 1 large cucumber)

2 cups diced vine-ripened tomatoes (about 3 medium tomatoes)

¼ cup olive oil

¾ cup freshly squeezed lemon juice (2½ to 3 lemons)

1 teaspoon ground sumac

1½ teaspoons salt

1 teaspoon black pepper

Soak the bulgur in the cold water for 2 hours until soft. Drain and then squeeze excess water from the bulgur using your hands or a paper towel. Combine all the ingredients in a large bowl and thoroughly stir together. Let marinate in the fridge for at least 30 minutes before serving.

POWER TIP: PARSLEY

Did you know that parsley contains three times as much vitamin C as an orange by weight, and twice as much iron as spinach? It's also a good source of iodine, copper, and manganese, and contains many flavonoid phytochemicals and volatile oils known to have anticarcinogenic properties. And, in one study published in the scientific journal *Nature*, researchers showed that vegetable consumption, particularly of parsley and onions, had a positive effect on bone density. Additionally, there've been positive indications from scientific studies that parsley might very well have blood sugar–stabilizing effects and also protect the body against diabetes-related damage. Parsley is a natural breath freshener and digestive aid, so it's probably highly fortunate that parsley appears in a tabouleh recipe, which also contains onions, scallions, and garlic.

Pineapple-Ginger Stir-Fry

Like many Thai dishes, this recipe combines sweet and savory flavors. Tangy, refreshing, and light, this stir-fry makes a great accompaniment to all sorts of dishes. Yield: 3 to 4 servings

1 tablespoon sesame oil

1 inch fresh ginger, peeled and julienned into ⅛-inch thick matchsticks (about 1 tablespoon)

¼ cup finely minced shallot (about 1 large shallot)

2 cups diced fresh pineapple

¾ cup diced green bell pepper (about ½ large pepper)

¾ cup diced red bell pepper (about ½ large pepper)

5 fresh, small Thai red chiles, stemmed, seeded, ribbed, and julienned into ⅛-inch-thick strips (about 1 tablespoon)

1 tablespoon fresh finely minced garlic (about 2 large cloves)

1 teaspoon salt

1 teaspoon ground black pepper

2 tablespoons soy sauce

1 tablespoon fresh pineapple juice

¼ cup sliced scallions, white and green parts, in ¼-inch rounds (about 2 large scallions)

1 tablespoon freshly squeezed lime juice

¼ cup julienned fresh basil, loosely packed

1 tablespoon coarsely chopped fresh cilantro, loosely packed

2 tablespoons crushed unsalted roasted peanuts

Heat the sesame oil in a large wok over high heat until glistening, then add the ginger and shallots and cook for 1 to 2 minutes, stirring frequently. Add the pineapple, green and red bell pepper, Thai chiles, and garlic, stirring occasionally. Season with salt and pepper from high above, for even distribution.

As soon as the fruit and vegetables become tender, stir in the soy sauce and pineapple juice. Then add the scallions and cook for 1 minute more. Remove from the heat. Stir in the lime juice and thoroughly combine. Garnish with the basil and cilantro, stirring everything together thoroughly, and transfer to plates. Sprinkle peanuts on top of each portion and serve.

Portuguese Black Rice

Black rice is a superfood rich in the antioxidant anthocyanin and is also an excellent source of fiber and vitamin E. It's much more nutritious than brown rice and even contains more antioxidants than blueberries! This dish is a good accompaniment for Piri Piri Chicken (page 74).   Yield: 4 servings

2 tablespoons extra-virgin olive oil

1 cup finely diced yellow onion (about ¾ large onion)

2 teaspoons finely minced garlic (about 4 cloves)

1 large bay leaf

1 cup black rice

3 cups water

6 tablespoons diced red bell pepper (about ½ medium bell pepper)

½ teaspoon salt, or to taste

¼ teaspoon red chile pepper flakes or ground black pepper (for less heat)

2 teaspoons paprika

2 tablespoons finely minced fresh cilantro

In a large saucepan, heat the olive oil over high heat until glistening. Then reduce the heat to low, add the onion, garlic, and bay leaf, and sauté until the onion is tender, about 5 minutes. Add the rice, turn up the heat to medium, and cook for 1 to 2 minutes, until the rice begins to crisp, stirring occasionally. Watch the pan carefully so the rice doesn't brown or burn. (This step is particularly important, as it cooks off the rice's starchy coating and prevents the grains from getting sticky and mushy when the liquid ingredients are added. The rice should be slightly crispy, but not browned. When ready, a translucent outline will form on its exterior.)

As soon as the rice crisps, quickly deglaze with water, stirring to break up the fond (the brown bits) from the bottom of the pan. Cover the pan and cook the rice, undisturbed, until it's al dente, 20 to 25 minutes. During the last 5 minutes of cooking, stir in the bell pepper, season with salt, red chile pepper flakes, and paprika, and continue to cook until the rice is tender but still slightly firm. Remove from the heat and discard the bay leaf with a slotted spoon. Fluff with a fork, then transfer to plates. Garnish each portion with ½ tablespoon cilantro. Serve immediately.

Mexican Egg Salad

Make no mistake about it, this egg salad is totally different from your average traditional egg salad. I use the term "egg salad" rather loosely here, as there's no mayo in this recipe, nor is it just eggs. Nonetheless it's still rich and creamy, and packed with flavor. And unlike most egg salads, it contains lots of fresh vegetables and tomatoes for added taste, texture, and nutritional value. Plus, in contrast to other versions, you can actually see and taste the eggs.

This is the kind of dish that's perfect for picnics, barbecues, and casual parties, because it takes very little effort to make. Even better, you can whip it up in a snap; it takes under 30 minutes to make and there's basically zero cooking involved aside from boiling the pota-toes and eggs.   Yield: 3 to 4 servings

SALAD

1 cup halved grape tomatoes (about 10 large grape tomatoes)

¼ cup scallions, white and green parts, sliced crosswise into ¼-inch-thick rounds (about 4 large scallions)

¼ cup finely minced fresh cilantro, tightly packed

½ tablespoon capers, drained, soaked in 2 tablespoons water for 10 minutes, and then drained again

6 to 8 cups lightly salted water, for boiling the potatoes

½ pound red-skinned potatoes, unpeeled and well-scrubbed (about 1 medium potato)

2 large hard-boiled eggs, peeled and sliced crosswise into ⅛-inch-thick rounds with an egg slicer

DRESSING

2 tablespoons extra-virgin olive oil

1 tablespoon freshly squeezed lime juice (from about ½ large lime)

1 teaspoon Dijon mustard

1 teaspoon ground cumin

1 teaspoon paprika

¼ teaspoon dried or ground oregano

⅛ teaspoon ground black pepper

⅛ teaspoon ground cayenne pepper

MAKE THE SALAD: Place the grape tomatoes, scallions, cilantro, and capers into a large bowl and set aside. Bring the lightly salted water to a rolling boil over high heat in a medium pot, about 8 minutes. Then gingerly place the potatoes into the pot of boiling water. Reduce the heat to medium-low, cover tightly with a lid, and simmer for 15 to 20 minutes, or until the potatoes are almost tender when pierced with a knife. Drain into a heatproof colander, then transfer the potatoes back into the pot and let them cool for at least 15 minutes. Set aside.

MAKE THE DRESSING: Meanwhile, pour all of the dressing ingredients into a blender or food processor, cover, and pulse until smooth and emulsified. Pour into the large bowl of vegetables and gently combine. Set aside. This will allow the solid ingredients some time to marinate in the dressing while you're waiting for the potatoes to cool.

When the potatoes are cool enough to handle but still warm, dice them into small, rough chunks while they're still in the pot. Then transfer the potatoes into the large bowl of vegetables. Toss well, then add the hard-boiled eggs and gently mix together with salad tongs. Cover, and refrigerate for a few hours (or even better, overnight) to allow the flavors to meld. Serve cold or at room temperature.

Chef's Notes: I like to leave the potato peels intact when adding the potatoes to the salad for added color, flavor, texture, and nutrients, but whether you'd like to do this is, of course, up to you. No additional salt is needed for this recipe. The capers provide sufficient salt.

Alternate Preparation Ideas: Instead of serving this recipe as a side dish, you could also use it as filling for a refreshingly new and totally different kind of egg salad sandwich.

Celery Remoulade

Celery is often taken for granted as something that's added to enhance the flavor of other ingredients, not as a featured dish on its own. This dish turns that notion on its head by transforming it into something far more exciting, while still letting its flavor shine through. Crunchy, light, and refreshing, this is the perfect side dish for summer! Yield: 6 to 8 servings

1 egg yolk

¾ teaspoon kosher salt

½ teaspoon ground black pepper

1 tablespoon Dijon mustard

1 tablespoon distilled white vinegar

3 tablespoons freshly squeezed lemon juice, divided

½ cup walnut oil

½ cup plain, nonfat Greek yogurt

1 tablespoon finely minced fresh tarragon

3 cups diced celery (about 7 large ribs)

1 cup peeled, diced Granny Smith apple (about ½ large apple)

2 tablespoons finely minced cornichons

2 tablespoons capers, rinsed, then soaked in ¼ cup water and drained

Whisk the egg, salt, pepper, and mustard in a deep, large mixing bowl until well combined. Add the vinegar and 1 tablespoon of the lemon juice, and briskly whisk together, slowly incorporating the walnut oil until the mixture emulsifies and begins to thicken. Refrigerate for 2 hours to allow mixture to thicken even more.

Remove from the fridge and add the Greek yogurt and remaining 2 tablespoons lemon juice. Whisk again, rapidly, until well combined. Add the tarragon and gently mix together. Refrigerate again.

Remove from the fridge and add the celery, apple, cornichons, and capers to the sauce, and thoroughly toss to coat all of the ingredients. Cover with plastic wrap and refrigerate for at least 3 hours before serving. (The longer you marinate it, the better it will taste!) Serve cold or at room temperature. Will keep up to 2 to 3 days in the fridge.

Chef's Notes: I know it might sound weird to combine celery with apple, but it's surprisingly good. Celery tends to be a bit bitter, and the sauce is also very tangy, so the apple really helps mellow out the flavor of this dish. It adds just a hint of natural sweetness. Both the apple and the celery have a crunchy texture, so they are the perfect complement for one another.

Don't be concerned about using a raw egg; the acidic components in the sauce (i.e., lemon juice and vinegar) "cold cook" all of the ingredients and tenderize the grated celery root to give it a nice texture.

Ginger-Garlic Baby Carrots

This simple but flavorful side dish is extremely versatile and goes with practically any entrée.   Yield: 3 to 4 servings

1 tablespoon finely minced fresh garlic (about 2 large cloves)

½ tablespoon peeled, finely minced fresh ginger (about a ½-inch piece)

¼ teaspoon salt

1 tablespoon extra-virgin olive oil

1 large fresh bay leaf

1 cup low-sodium vegetable broth

2 cups sliced baby carrots, cut crosswise into ¼-inch rounds

¼ cup sliced scallions, in ¼-inch rounds

1 to 2 tablespoons coarsely chopped fresh flat-leaf parsley

Mash the garlic, ginger, and salt together into a smooth paste using a mortar and pestle. Then, in a large (12 to 13-inch) sauté pan, heat the olive oil over medium-high heat until glistening. Then, reduce the heat to low, add the garlic-ginger paste and bay leaf, and sauté for 5 minutes, or until the garlic no longer smells raw. Deglaze with vegetable broth, stirring to loosen the fond (brown bits on the bottom of the pan), add the carrots, cover with a lid, and simmer for 20 minutes, or until the water has almost completely evaporated. Remove from the heat and allow to cool. Add the scallions and stir to combine thoroughly. Garnish with parsley and serve.

Cauliflower Mash with Rosemary & Roasted Garlic

Cauliflower mash is a great, nutritious alternative to mashed potatoes, and goes amazingly well with all sorts of dishes, whether it's fish, chicken, turkey, beef, or lamb or even other vegetables. This recipe contains omega-3-rich walnut oil, instead of butter or olive oil, which is great for reducing post-exercise inflammation. Serving this dish is also a great way to sneak a vegetable into your meal. Yield: 4 to 6 servings

medium garlic clove, unpeeled

1 tablespoon walnut oil or extra-virgin olive oil, plus a little bit more for roasting garlic

1 (1-pound) head cauliflower, quartered and broken into florets

1 teaspoon dried rosemary

¼ teaspoon paprika

¼ teaspoon salt

⅛ teaspoon ground black pepper

⅛ teaspoon ground nutmeg

Preheat a toaster oven to 400°F. Place the unpeeled garlic clove onto a small piece of aluminum foil, then drizzle with a small amount of walnut oil. Completely wrap the garlic in foil, then place onto the toaster oven tray and roast for 25 to 30 minutes, or until golden brown.

Meanwhile, place a steamer basket into a large pot, fill it with water until it reaches the bottom of the basket, and then bring to a rolling boil. Add the cauliflower florets, cover, and boil for 15 to 20 minutes, or until the cauliflower is tender. Turn off the burner, then pour the cauliflower into a colander and drain. Let it rest there for 1 to 2 minutes to dry.

When the garlic has finished roasting, remove it from the toaster oven and let cool for 5 minutes, or until cool to the touch. Then peel and mash. Measure out ¾ teaspoon of the mashed garlic, and place this amount into a food processor, followed by the steamed cauliflower. Add the remaining ingredients, and process until fluffy. Serve immediately.

Chef's Notes: Due to the quantity of cauliflower and/or the size of your food processor, you may have to process the cauliflower a few florets at a time, and then add the remaining ingredients after that.

Asian-Style Jicama Slaw

This crunchy and refreshing side dish isn't your usual "slaw" recipe. Its spicy and sweet flavors work with all sorts of dishes, including stir-fries, barbecued foods, and rice dishes. It's perfect for a barbecue or picnic, complementing everything from juicy burgers and hot dogs to grilled chicken and vegetable kebabs. Jicama slaw also goes exceptionally well with spicy Mexican dishes like fajitas or burritos, or Mediterranean/Middle Eastern foods. It's particularly good mixed with cold noodles. Jicama has a crisp, clean flavor with a crunchy texture. Due to its high-fiber content, it's a very filling selection and is often credited as being a natural "weight loss" food. Yield: 12 servings

SLAW INGREDIENTS

2 cups jicama, peeled and then shredded or julienned (about 1 large jicama bulb)

1 cup purple cabbage, shredded

1 cup baby carrots, shredded

1 cup celery, shredded (about 1 large stalk)

1 cup red bell pepper, shredded (about ¾ large pepper)

1 cup scallions including the green stems, sliced thinly on the bias (about 7 to 8 large scallions)

½ cup toasted almonds, slivered (or crushed toasted peanuts, whichever you prefer)

¼ cup fresh cilantro, finely minced (optional)

DRESSING INGREDIENTS

¼ cup sesame oil

2 tablespoons soy sauce

1 tablespoon rice wine vinegar

2 tablespoons honey

¼ cup freshly squeezed lime juice (about 1 to 1½ large limes)

½ tablespoon lime zest

1 tablespoon grated ginger (about a 1-inch piece)

1 tablespoon minced garlic (about 2 cloves)

⅛ teaspoon crushed red chili pepper flakes

⅛ teaspoon freshly ground black pepper

OPTIONAL INGREDIENTS

1 cup cooked chow mein noodles, cooled to room temperature

½ cup daikon radish, peeled and shredded

½ cup cucumber, stripe-peeled and cut into matchsticks/cubes (about ½ large cucumber)

½ cup avocado, peeled, pitted, and chopped (about ½ large avocado)

To prepare the shredded vegetables, use a food processor with a shredder blade. You can also use the food processor to make the dressing. Thoroughly toss together the slaw ingredients and dressing in a large serving bowl. Chill in the refrigerator for at least 15 to 30 minutes before serving, to allow flavors to develop. Serve and enjoy!

Chef's Notes: When buying jicama, look for vegetables with unblemished skin that are relatively dense in weight for their size. Unpeeled jicama will keep in the refrigerator for up to 3 weeks.

Pilau (Aromatic Basmati Rice)

This aromatic side dish fills your entire kitchen with its lovely fragrance and just makes your whole house smell wonderful. And the best part! It's super easy to make and takes only 15 minutes to cook. You can either make it in a sauce pot or, if you have one, a rice steamer; either way, there's no slicing or dicing. Seriously, there's almost zero kitchen prep. You get maximum flavor for minimum effort.   Yield: 4 servings

1 to 1½ teaspoons saffron

2 tablespoons plain soy milk

1 cup brown basmati rice

1 tablespoon extra-virgin olive oil

1 large bay leaf

3 (3-inch) whole cinnamon sticks, broken in half

5 whole cloves

14 whole green cardamom pods

1 teaspoon fennel seeds

1 teaspoon cumin seeds

2 cups water, or more as needed

1 teaspoon ground coriander

½ teaspoon ground ginger

¼ teaspoon ground turmeric

¼ teaspoon onion powder

¼ teaspoon plus a pinch salt, or to taste

⅛ teaspoon ground black pepper, or to taste

1½ tablespoons fresh cilantro

STOVETOP DIRECTIONS: Combine the saffron and soy milk in a small bowl and stir to combine. For a less pronounced saffron flavor, use just 1 teaspoon saffron threads. Set aside.

Wash the rice by placing it into a large strainer, running it under cold water, and then swishing it around until the water runs clear. (This will remove any excess starch coating from the rice). Use your fingers to swirl the rice around in the strainer to ensure it is thoroughly washed. Drain and set aside over a small bowl.

Heat the olive oil in a medium saucepan over high heat until glistening. Add the bay leaf, cinnamon sticks, cloves, cardamom pods, fennel seeds, and cumin seeds, and "flash-fry" for 60 seconds to release the spices' essence, covering the pan with a splatter screen to avoid being burned by sputtering oil. Reduce the heat to low, add the rice, and cook for 1 minute more, stirring occasionally. Watch the pot closely so the rice doesn't burn; it will be a light golden brown when ready. (This is done to crisp the rice and keep it from getting soggy as it cooks while immersed in water.) Add the water, coriander, ginger, turmeric, onion powder, salt, and pepper, and stir. Cover with a tight-fitting lid and simmer for 15 minutes for al dente rice, or until the water has been completely absorbed. (Check on the rice after 15 minutes to make sure it hasn't cooked down too quickly. If it needs to cook for longer, add water as necessary.) Remove from the heat and let the rice rest for about 10 minutes. With a spoon, remove the bay leaf, cinnamon sticks, cloves, and cardamom seeds and discard. Fluff the rice with a fork, then sprinkle in the cilantro and stir just until combined. Divide into 4 portions, and serve immediately.

RICE STEAMER DIRECTIONS: Wash the rice by placing it into a large strainer, running it under cold water, and then swishing it around until the water runs clear. (This will remove any excess starch coating the rice). Use your fingers to swirl the rice around in the strainer to ensure it is thoroughly washed. Drain and set aside (over a small bowl).

Add the olive oil to the rice steamer, followed by the rice, water, and all the spices except for the cilantro, in that particular order. Stir once to combine, and cover with the inner steamer tray and lid. Cook for 15 to 20 minutes for al dente rice, or until the water has been completely absorbed (see note). (Check on the rice after 15 minutes to make sure it hasn't cooked down too quickly and/or burned on the bottom. If it needs to cook for longer, add water as necessary.) If your steamer doesn't have a timer with an auto shut-off feature, turn it off when the rice has finished cooking. Let the rice rest for about 10 minutes. With a spoon, remove the bay leaf, cinnamon sticks, cloves, and cardamom seeds and discard. Fluff the rice with a fork, then sprinkle in the cilantro and stir just until combined. Divide into 4 portions, and serve immediately.

Chef's Notes: I use a Japanese rice steamer, Zojirushi brand, which in my humble opinion is the gold standard for rice steamers. Many, if not most, rice steamers have a built-in timer with an auto shut-off feature; there's usually a button you can press to cook the rice that will release with a pop when the rice is done. Typically, this will take 15 to 20 minutes, although you can cook it for longer if you like your rice a bit softer than al dente.

Roasted Butternut Squash & Corn

The nutrients in butternut squash have been shown to improve endurance, muscle tissue repair, and metabolism. Yield: 4 servings

1½ pounds unpeeled butternut squash, quartered

1 medium red bell pepper

1 medium jalapeño pepper

½ small unpeeled red onion

2 large garlic cloves, unpeeled

1 tablespoon extra-virgin olive oil

½ cup fresh or frozen corn kernels

1 tablespoon freshly squeezed lime juice

½ tablespoon ground cumin

½ teaspoon red chile pepper flakes

¼ teaspoon salt, or to taste

2 tablespoons finely minced cilantro

4 ounces feta cheese, crumbled (optional)

Preheat the oven to 400°F and cover an 11 x 17-inch baking sheet with aluminum foil. Place the squash, bell pepper, jalapeño pepper, red onion, and garlic onto the prepared baking sheet, and brush them all over with olive oil. The vegetables have different roasting times, so while the total roasting time is 40 minutes, you'll rotate and remove various vegetables at different times, until tender. Of course, the smallest items cook the fastest: The garlic cooks in 10 minutes, the jalapeño in 20 minutes, the squash in 30 minutes, and the red bell pepper in 40 minutes.

To simplify the process, use the following time table:

AT THE 5-MINUTE MARK	Flip over the garlic.
AT THE 10-MINUTE MARK	Remove the garlic, flip over the jalapeño and red onion, and rotate the red bell pepper one quarter turn.
AT THE 15-MINUTE MARK	Flip over the squash.
AT THE 20-MINUTE MARK	Remove the jalapeño and red onion, and rotate the red bell pepper another quarter turn.
AT THE 30-MINUTE MARK	Remove the squash, which should be tender and golden brown, and rotate the red bell pepper another quarter turn.
AT THE 40 MINUTE-MARK	Remove the red bell pepper, which should be blistered and slightly charred.

While the vegetables are roasting, bring a small pot of water to a rolling boil, add the corn, and cook until tender, 4 to 5 minutes tops. Drain into a colander, transfer to a large serving bowl, and set aside to cool.

When the vegetables are cool to the touch (after at least 10 to 15 minutes of resting), peel and dice them into bite-size pieces. The squash should be diced into 1¼-inch pieces or smaller. Place all the cut-up vegetables into the serving bowl. Add the lime juice, cumin, chile flakes, salt, cilantro, and feta cheese (if using), and toss. Serve warm or at room temperature.

Wilted Mustard Greens

Mustard greens are high in vitamins A, C, and E, folate, manganese, and are a great source of fiber. Serve with Almond-Crusted Haddock (page 66).   Yield: 4 servings

1 tablespoon extra-virgin olive oil

½ cup finely minced shallot (about 2 medium shallots)

1 tablespoon finely minced garlic (about 2 large cloves)

¼ cup water

1 pound mustard greens, chopped into bite-size pieces (about 6 cups)

¼ teaspoon salt

¼ teaspoon ground black pepper, or to taste

1 tablespoon freshly squeezed lemon juice, or to taste

In a large (12 to 13-inch) sauté pan, heat the olive oil over high heat until glistening. Then reduce the heat to low, add the shallots and garlic, and sauté until tender, about 5 minutes. Deglaze with water, stirring to loosen the fond (the brown bits) from the bottom of the pan. Cook until the liquid is reduced by half, then add the mustard greens, and season with salt and pepper. Gently wilt the greens on low heat for 3 to 5 minutes. Remove from the heat, drain excess the liquid in a colander, and set aside. Let cool slightly. Drizzle with lemon juice and serve.

Swoon-Worthy Sweet Potatoes

Sweet potatoes are the perfect carbo-loading food for endurance athletes.   Yield: 4 servings

1 pound sweet potatoes, unpeeled, scrubbed, and diced into bite-size pieces (about 2 medium potatoes; about 3 cups diced)

3 tablespoons walnut oil

2 tablespoons freshly squeezed lemon juice

1 tablespoon paprika

1 teaspoon cracked black pepper, or to taste

1 teaspoon coarse sea salt

2 tablespoons finely minced fresh rosemary

1½ tablespoons finely minced garlic (about 3 large cloves)

½ cup finely minced shallot (about 2 large shallots)

2 tablespoons finely minced fresh oregano (about 1 large sprig)

2 tablespoons finely minced fresh thyme (about 2 large sprigs)

2 tablespoons finely minced fresh flat-leaf parsley

Place all the ingredients except for the oregano, thyme, and parsley into a large bowl in the order shown. Toss with a spatula until the potatoes are fully coated. Next, heat a large (12 to 13-inch) sauté pan for about 30 seconds over medium-high heat, then reduce heat to medium and add the sweet potato mixture, evenly distributing the potatoes across the pan. Cook for 10 minutes, then add the oregano and thyme and cook for another 10 minutes, stirring frequently. Add the parsley and cook for 2 to 3 minutes, or until potatoes are tender and golden brown. Remove from the heat, garnish with sprigs of fresh parsley, and serve immediately.

Snacks

Baked Sweet Potato Chips

Sweet potatoes are a fantastic source of long-lasting energy, as well as a high-satiety food that helps stabilize blood sugar. They're packed with phytonutrients, particularly beta-carotene and vitamins A and C. Yield: 3 cups

1 large sweet potato (about 1½ pounds), unpeeled and thinly sliced crosswise into wafer-thin ($1/16$-inch) rounds (about 3 cups)

1 tablespoon paprika

½ teaspoon kosher (or sea) salt

½ teaspoon garlic powder

¼ teaspoon onion powder

¼ teaspoon ground black pepper

¼ cup extra-virgin olive oil

Preheat the oven to 375°F, and line 2 large 11 x 17-inch baking sheets with aluminum foil or parchment paper (for easy cleanup).

Place the sweet potato slices into a large, deep bowl. In a medium bowl, thoroughly combine the paprika, salt, garlic powder, onion powder, and pepper, then sprinkle over the sweet potatoes and toss. Drizzle the extra-virgin olive oil across the bowl to evenly distribute. While wearing rubber or latex gloves to keep your hands clean an oil-free, mix everything together with your hands until well-blended, thoroughly massaging the spice and oil mixture into the sweet potatoes until they've been completely and evenly coated. Spread the sweet potato slices in a single layer onto the prepared baking sheets. Try not to let the slices touch, as this will create crispier edges. Bake for 15 minutes, or until crisp, completely dry, and golden brown, especially around the edges. Remove from the oven and transfer to a wire rack to cool. Allow the chips to completely cool before transferring into any kind of closed storage container. (Otherwise, they'll become soggy.)

Chef's Notes: Vegetable chips tend to bake quickly, so check the chips about halfway through, then again around the 15-minute marker, to make sure they don't burn. When done, the chips should be golden brown. Be sure the chips are completely dry—not just crisp—after they are removed from the oven. To test for doneness, gently shake the tray after removing from the oven; if the chips make a rattling noise and release easily, they are done. For best results, slice the sweet potatoes with a mandoline (see page 158).

Date & Almond Clusters

This no-bake recipe takes the classic Mediterranean combo of dates and almonds and turns it into a new bite-size snack. Be sure your dates are super fresh and soft to avoid damaging your food processor.   Yield: 12 clusters

1 cup Deglet Noor (common) dates, pitted

¼ cup slivered almonds

½ cup almond meal

1 teaspoon pure vanilla extract

⅛ teaspoon salt

12 raw unsalted almonds

Place all the ingredients minus the whole raw almonds into a food processor and pulse until well combined. Spread a large piece of waxed paper across a large, clean plate and set aside. Wet your hands first, then roll a piece of the dough in your palms to form a half-dollar-sized ball and place onto the waxed paper. Repeat this process until all the dough has been rolled into balls. Then rewet your hands and flatten each ball into a disc. Press an almond into each cluster, then refrigerate for 10 to 15 minutes to solidify. Serve and enjoy! Refrigerate any leftovers in an airtight container.

Toasted Chili-Lime Pumpkin Seeds

These pumpkin seeds are the perfect grab-and-go snack for the busy athlete. You'll want to make this treat again and again since it's not only tasty but so quick and easy to make!   Yield: 1 cup

1 cup shelled, unsalted pumpkin seeds

2 tablespoons freshly squeezed lime juice

½ tablespoon Mexican chili powder

¼ teaspoon garlic powder

¼ teaspoon salt

Place the pumpkin seeds into a bowl and pour the lime juice on top. Mix with a spatula until the seeds are completely covered with lime juice. Then fold in the chili powder, garlic powder, and salt until well combined. Spread out the pumpkin seeds in a single layer on an aluminum foil–coated toaster tray (for easy cleanup) and cook in a toaster oven at 200°F for 15 to 20 minutes, or until the seeds turn a very light golden brown. (Cooking at a low temperature helps to preserve their healthy oils.) After about 10 minutes, be sure to gently rattle the tray a bit, or simply move the seeds around with a heatproof utensil. This will keep them from sticking to the aluminum foil. Watch the oven carefully, as the seeds tend to burn easily. Let cool. Serve immediately or store in a non-reactive, airtight container for future use.

Sweet & Salty Peanut Butter Crunch Bars

Who doesn't love peanut butter? It doesn't take much to fill you up, which is why it's the perfect food to incorporate into a snack. This recipe's a total no-brainer. You basically just toss together a bunch of ingredients and bake them. And that makes it a lot easier to eat healthfully, as it's not only easy to make but you'll now have ready-made snacks that can be taken anywhere. Use them as pre- or post-exercise energy bars, or for refueling while you're out on the trail. It's packed with a combination of all natural carbs and protein to provide both balance and lasting energy.　Yield: 24 bars

DRY INGREDIENTS

2 cups unsalted dry-roasted peanuts

1 cup oats, processed into flour in a food processor

½ cup almond meal

½ cup ground flaxseed

½ cup brown or white sesame seeds

1 cup shredded unsweetened coconut, shredded

½ cup dry nonfat milk or soy milk powder

1 teaspoon salt

2 teaspoons baking soda

WET INGREDIENTS

1 cup unsalted reduced-fat, no-sugar-added crunchy peanut butter

½ cup honey

½ cup pure maple syrup

1½ tablespoons pure vanilla extract

¼ cup extra virgin coconut oil

Preheat the oven to 350°F. Spread the peanuts onto an 11 x 17-inch baking sheet in a single, even layer, and toast in the oven for 15 to 20 minutes until light golden brown. (Nuts burn easily, so be sure to check them for doneness at regular intervals.) Remove from the oven and let cool for at least 10 minutes.

Mix together all the remaining dry ingredients in a food processor and pulse until combined. Transfer the dry ingredients to the bowl of a stand mixer or a large mixing bowl. Pour in all wet ingredients and mix on low speed, or fold in with a spatula. Combine just until the dry ingredients have become moist. Turn off the mixer. Next, add peanuts and gently mix together, being very careful not to press down on them too hard. (You don't want to mash them into oblivion.) Set aside.

Line an 11 x 17-inch baking sheet with parchment paper. Using a sturdy rubber or silicone spatula, scoop out the mixture from the bowl into the prepared pan, and spread it completely across the baking sheet to a ¾-inch thickness. Press down to compact the mixture a bit. Bake for 15 to 20 minutes, or until firm and golden brown. Watch the oven carefully to make sure bars do not become brittle and overly dry, and/or burned.

When ready, remove from the oven and place onto a wire cooling rack or heatproof trivet. Let cool for at least 5 minutes before dividing into bars, but don't wait too long either, or they'll be more difficult to cut into. Be sure to cut into them while they're still warm. Using a sharp knife, divide into 24 rectangular bars. Keep the bars in the pan, cover, and refrigerate for at least 1 to 2 hours to set.

Chef's Notes: Any bars you won't be consuming right away can be wrapped in waxed paper and then placed into a tightly sealed plastic container or reinforced, zip-top plastic bags for on-the-go snacking; just make sure they're completely cool before wrapping them in waxed paper. (Or, alternatively, wrap in waxed paper, place into plastic freezer bags, and freeze. These bars freeze exceptionally well.)

Olive Hummus

Hummus is one of those perfect snack foods. It tastes great with toasted pita chips, lavash, carrots, babaganoush, tabouleh, and/or stuffed grape leaves. It can be eaten as a snack, appetizer, or as the main course of a meal. It's traditionally served as part of a mezze (a small selection of dishes eaten for breakfast, lunch, or dinner throughout the Levant region, the Mediterranean, and elsewhere) or piled into a pita, along with tabouleh and falafel, and topped with a small drizzle of tahini. You can also use it as a sandwich filling or burger topping. For best results, in this recipe use a pure ground sesame tahini, like Joyva brand. Be sure to stir the tahini first before measuring; the oil usually rises to the top, so you'll need to thoroughly blend it.

Serve with crudités and Za'atar Crackers with Sesame, Cumin, Caraway, & Nigella Seeds (page 138) or Tabouleh (page 117).   Yield: About 16 ounces

1 (15.5-ounce) can or 2 cups chickpeas, drained and rinsed

1 tablespoon finely minced garlic (about 2 large cloves)

3 tablespoons tahini

¼ cup nonfat yogurt

3 tablespoons freshly squeezed lemon juice (from about 1 lemon)

1 tablespoon grated lemon zest (from about 1 lemon)

1 tablespoon paprika

1 teaspoon ground cumin

½ teaspoon salt

⅛ teaspoon ground black pepper

½ cup pitted and diced kalamata olives

a few sprinkles of paprika, for garnish

a small amount of extra-virgin olive oil, drizzled on top, for garnish

In a food processor, toss all ingredients except the olives, paprika, and olive oil into a food processor and purée until smooth. (If you like your hummus a bit chunkier, simply don't blend for as long.) Fold in the diced olives and evenly distribute. Using a spatula, scoop out the hummus into a nonreactive container with a lid and refrigerate until ready to serve.

When ready to serve, spread the hummus on a plate, and lightly sprinkle with paprika. Create a shallow well, and pour a very small amount (½ to 1 tablespoon) of olive oil into the well. Or, alternatively, just drizzle olive oil around in a spiral.

Chef's Notes: For a spicier hummus, add a dash of ground cayenne pepper. Homemade hummus can be stored in the refrigerator for up to 3 days, and can be kept in the freezer for up to 1 month. After defrosting or removing from refrigerator, add a little olive oil or water if it appears to be too dry.

Whipped Ricotta Cream with Fresh Berries

Fresh and light, this dish is perfect all by itself.   Yield: 4 to 6 servings

2 cups part-skim ricotta

¼ cup honey

1 teaspoon pure vanilla extract

1 tablespoon freshly squeezed lemon juice

1 teaspoon grated lemon zest

½ cup hulled, sliced strawberries

½ cup blueberries

1 tablespoon whole fresh mint leaves, for garnish

Blend ricotta, honey, vanilla, and lemon juice and zest in a food processor until smooth, about 2 minutes. Refrigerate for at least 2 to 3 hours before serving Divide into equal portions, and top with fresh blueberries, sliced strawberries, and mint leaves.

No-Bake Chocolate-Cherry-Almond Energy Bites

These nutritious, satisfying, and naturally sweet bite-sized treats make great pre- or post-workout snacks. They're also the perfect portion size for a mid-day snack or even a mini dessert. Take them with you on the go when you need something quick and healthy to pop into your mouth.   Yield: 38 to 40 energy bites

¼ cup plus 2 tablespoons slivered almonds, divided

½ cup rolled oats, finely ground into flour in a food processor

2 tablespoons unsweetened cocoa powder

1 cup reduced-fat almond butter (be sure to use the kind with salt)

¼ cup honey

1 cup sugar-free dried cherries, densely packed

In a food processor, coarsely grind ¼ cup of the slivered almonds with 3 to 4 quick pulses. Transfer to a small bowl and set aside.

Combine the oat flour, remaining 2 tablespoons slivered almonds, and cocoa powder in a food processor and process until just incorporated. Then add the almond butter and honey and pulse until smooth and fully blended. Add the cherries and pulse only until just combined.

Transfer the dough to a clean surface and roll into bite-size balls (about the size of a quarter) using the palms of your hands. Then dip each ball into the small bowl containing the ground almonds and roll around in the bowl to completely cover in nuts. Place each ball on an 11 x 17-inch waxed paper–covered baking sheet as you complete them, spacing them evenly apart from each other. Refrigerate for 15 minutes to solidify. Eat and enjoy! Refrigerate any leftovers.

Popcorn Snack Bars

What?! A candy-coated popcorn snack bar that's actually GOOD for you?! Are you kidding me?! Does such a thing even exist? Salty and sweet, and yes, healthy, this snack covers all of the bases. It's got all-natural carbs, healthy fats, and protein, omega-3s and -6s, is an abundant source of energy, and heck, it even fights germs. It's sort of like Cracker Jack's healthier, badass cousin. Plus, it also makes a great gift for the holidays or other special occasions! Yield: 10 bars

8 cups plain, freshly air-popped popcorn (about 3 tablespoons popping corn kernels)

⅓ cup raw unsalted almonds

⅓ cup honey

⅓ cup maple syrup

½ teaspoon salt

1 tablespoon walnut oil

1 teaspoon pure vanilla extract

½ teaspoon baking soda

⅓ cup raw unsalted cashews

⅓ cup raw unsalted pecan halves

Preheat a toaster oven to 350°F. Pour the plain, freshly air-popped popcorn into a large heatproof bowl. Pick out and discard any unpopped kernels. Set aside. Spread the almonds onto an aluminum foil–covered toaster oven tray and bake until golden brown and fragrant, about 10 minutes, opening the oven after the first 5 minutes to stir them a bit. (Nuts burn easily, so watch them carefully as they toast.) Transfer the nuts to a separate heatproof bowl and let them cool for 5 to 10 minutes.

While the nuts are cooling, preheat a conventional oven to 350°F and line a 9 x 13-inch baking dish with parchment paper. Then, add the honey, maple syrup, and salt to a large saucepan, stirring once to combine, and then simmer, undisturbed, over low heat. (Watch it carefully so that it doesn't boil over.) Cook until the honey dissolves, about 5 minutes. Stir in the walnut oil in the last 30 seconds. Remove from the heat, then stir in the vanilla and baking soda, the latter of which will cause the mixture to foam. Quickly add all of the nuts and stir until fully coated with syrup.

Using a heatproof spatula, immediately transfer the nuts and any remaining syrup to the bowl with the popcorn and mix together rapidly until the popcorn and nuts are completely covered in syrup. Then swiftly transfer the mixture to the prepared baking sheet. Using the heatproof spatula, firmly press the mixture into the baking sheet, evenly distributing it. Make sure there are no gaps anywhere and that the mixture is of a uniform thickness. Bake for 7 to 8 minutes, or until the bars have solidified and become golden brown.

Let the bars fully cool, then refrigerate for 1 hour to further solidify. Cut into 10 uniformly sized bars, slicing once lengthwise (down the center of the 13-inch side), and then 4 times crosswise (equidistantly down the 9-inch side). Serve and enjoy!

Chef's Notes: It's best to consume these snack bars within 1 to 2 days of making them. Otherwise, they'll become sticky and will crumble fairly easily while you're eating them, which make for some very messy snacking. (More popcorn will probably hit the floor than your mouth.) If you're not going to eat them right away, then be sure to store the bars in an airtight container to keep them fresh.

After the syrup has finished cooking, do not delay any of the steps immediately following, from the moment you remove it from the stovetop up until the instant after you've just pressed the syrup-coated popcorn and nuts into the baking sheet. Otherwise, the syrup will begin to harden and will make the popcorn and nut mixture difficult to handle.

Za'atar Crackers with Sesame, Cumin, Caraway, & Nigella Seeds

This is a supereasy and delicious high-protein snack that goes well with all sorts of condiments, particularly the Olive Hummus on page 134.   Yield: About 30 crackers

CRACKER DOUGH

½ cup ground flaxseed, divided

1 cup almond meal

1 large egg

1 teaspoon baking soda

¼ teaspoon kosher salt

2 tablespoons water

¼ cup brown or white sesame seeds

2 tablespoons nigella seeds

1 tablespoon caraway seeds

½ tablespoon cumin seeds

ZA'ATAR SPICE MIX

1 tablespoon fresh thyme

1 tablespoon fresh oregano, finely minced and densely packed

1 tablespoon ground sumac

salt, to taste (omit if the sumac you purchased already contains salt)

Preheat the oven to 375°F. Line an 11 x 17-inch baking sheet with parchment paper and dust it with ¼ cup of the ground flaxseed.

Place the almond meal, egg, remaining ¼ cup ground flaxseed, za'atar spice mix ingredients, and the baking soda, salt, and water in a food processor and pulse until well combined. Add the sesame, nigella, caraway, and cumin seeds until just combined.

Transfer the dough to a flat, clean surface that's been covered in parchment. Place another piece of parchment on top of the dough and press down on top of it with a rolling pin until flattened. Then roll out the dough until it's ⅛ inch thick. Peel off the top sheet of parchment paper and cut the dough into 1 to 1½-inch-wide strips. (If you've rolled out particularly long strips, it's a good idea to also make a horizontal cut across the center of the flattened dough, so that the dough strips aren't too long and unwieldy to transfer to the baking sheet.)

Slide a long spatula underneath each strip of dough and transfer it to the prepared baking sheet, spacing the strips evenly apart. (Depending upon how you've rolled out the dough, you may have to bake them in batches or use two baking trays.) Bake for about 10 minutes, or until golden brown.

Chef's Notes: You can also prep the dough in advance and either refrigerate or freeze it until you're ready to make the crackers.

Healthy Homemade Trail Mix

This recipe is so easy to make. Take it with you when you need a quick, portable snack before or after your endurance workouts. It's nutritious and fiber-rich and will keep you going up those hills. Lots of trail mixes are falsely advertised as healthy even though they are packed with sugar, fat, and even processed ingredients. So, when you make trail mix at home, you can control what goes into it and keep it healthy.   Yield: 4 (½-cup) servings

½ tablespoon extra-virgin coconut oil, for the pan

½ cup rolled oats

¼ cup unsalted shelled pumpkin seeds

2 tablespoons roasted unsalted cashews

2 tablespoons raw unsalted almonds

2 tablespoons unsweetened shredded coconut

2 tablespoons pineapple juice

1 tablespoon honey

1 tablespoon maple syrup

½ teaspoon pure vanilla extract

1 teaspoon ground cinnamon

¼ teaspoon ground nutmeg

¼ teaspoon allspice

⅛ teaspoon ground cloves

¼ teaspoon salt

¼ cup golden raisins

¼ cup dried cherries, cranberries, or strawberries

Preheat the oven to 325°F and lightly coat a baking sheet with coconut oil. In a small bowl, thoroughly combine all the remaining ingredients except for the raisins and dried berries. Mix until the dry ingredients have become moist. Evenly spread the mixture onto the prepared baking sheet and bake for 45 to 60 minutes, stirring after 25 minutes to ensure even baking. Watch carefully to make sure it doesn't burn. When ready, remove the trail mix from the oven. Allow to cool, breaking it apart while still slightly warm. Toss with the dried fruit and serve.

Chef's Notes: You could also add other types of nuts and dried fruit, like walnuts, hazelnuts, pecans, sliced dried apricots, apples, and/or peaches. Or, all-natural, homemade banana chips, made in a dehydrator (without any refined sugar), would also work as well.

Desserts

--- **Creamy Coconut Kheer (Indian Rice Pudding)** ---

Kheer is a wonderfully fragrant Indian rice pudding that's commonly served in many Indian restaurants. Most kheer recipes typically call for lots of cream or whole milk, but of course this recipe is the healthy version, so it doesn't contain either. Instead, I've used coconut milk, which, most notably, contains healthy fats that increase the rate of fat oxidation to provide an immediately available source of energy for athletes.

This dish is a little bit different than the standard variety in a few other ways: Instead of traditional basmati rice, it uses black rice, a superfood that's naturally sweet and unusually high in antioxidants, fiber, and protein. This kheer also has a ton of vitamins (especially vitamin E) and minerals (like iron, potassium, and magnesium) and is unusually rich in amino acids, the building blocks of lean muscle mass, All of these sports performance benefits make this dish an athlete's dream come true.

It also contains a plethora of fragrant ingredients, a wonderful, heady combination that'll make your kitchen smell divine. Get ready for a rich, complex, and intensely flavorful experience for your taste buds. This all natural, no-sugar-added pudding is, quite literally, as sweet as pie.   Yield: 5 servings

½ teaspoon saffron threads, crushed

½ cup black sticky rice

2 tablespoons slivered almonds

2 tablespoons unsalted shelled pistachios, plus more for garnish

1 (13.5-ounce) can coconut milk

1 cup water

½ teaspoon ground cardamom

1½ tablespoons honey

½ teaspoon rose water (optional)

⅛ teaspoon salt, or to taste

Soak the saffron threads in 3 tablespoons hot water for ideally 2 hours, or at least 30 minutes. Thoroughly wash the rice. Place it in a bowl with enough water to cover, soak for 30 minutes, then drain. Crush the almonds and pistachios coarsely using a mortar and pestle (or place onto a clean surface, cover with plastic wrap, and smash with the side of a knife) and set aside.

Pour the coconut milk and water into a large pot over high heat, cover, and bring to a boil. Add the rice, including the drained liquid, saffron, and cardamom. Cover and bring to a boil once more. Then reduce the heat to low and simmer for about 40 minutes, or until the rice is tender and almost all of the water has been absorbed. The rice should be tender but still slightly firm. Be careful not to overcook the rice or it'll be mushy and unpalatable. In the last 2 minutes of cooking, add the honey, rose water, if using, and salt, and stir until the honey is fully dissolved. Then add the almonds and pistachios. Spoon the rice pudding into small bowls and garnish each portion with crushed pistachios. Serve either warm or at room temperature.

Chef's Notes: Please note, this pudding has a short shelf life, and will last for only about a day. If you can't find unsalted pistachios, use the shelled salted ones but then omit the salt. Saffron can be soaked for much longer, anywhere from 2 to 12 hours, so you can also soak the saffron overnight. The longer it steeps, the more intense the saffron flavor will be.

Be sure to use Chinese sticky black rice and not wild rice. (Wild rice is a dark color, but trust me, it's not what you want to use for this pudding. The taste of wild rice is woody and savory, and totally wrong for a dish like this. Furthermore, wild rice isn't even technically considered to be rice.) Also, since this pudding is very sweet, it's a good idea to balance the sweetness by serving it with something plain or mild tasting, like a cup of herbal tea or a glass of milk.

Badass Brownies with Chocolate Fudge Frosting & Raspberry Swirl

You won't believe your eyes and taste buds when you bite into these brownies! They taste like real, honest-to-goodness brownies without resorting to the standard unhealthy ingredients—no refined sugar or butter, and the brownie batter is extremely low in fat. What little fat there is comes from soy and the almond butter in the frosting, both of which contain healthy unsaturated fats. The raspberries in this dish are an excellent source of antioxidants and omega-3s, containing the highest amount of omega-3s of any whole fruit, while the almond butter contains omega-6s. Plus, believe it or not, the cocoa powder provides a decent amount of protein, at 17 grams per cup!

Since fudge brownies are so rich and dense, it won't take much to fill you up. Even if you have big eyes, it shouldn't be very hard to eat them in moderation. So the next time you're having a sweets craving, try these in place of processed, sugary foods. They also make a great treat for parties, and they taste so much like the real deal that your guests won't even know that they're healthy.   Yield: 20 brownies

BATTER

1 cup Medjool dates, pitted and tightly packed (10 to 12 dates)

¾ cup boiling water, for soaking the dates

1 cup oats, processed into a fine powder in a food processor (homemade oat flour)

5 tablespoons unsweetened cocoa powder

2 teaspoons baking soda

2 tablespoons honey

1 cup unsweetened plain soy milk

RASPBERRY SAUCE

½ cup water

1 cup fresh or frozen raspberries, mashed (with a fork)

Icing:

½ cup unsweetened cocoa powder

¼ cup almond butter

¼ cup light silken tofu

5 tablespoons honey

2 tablespoons unsweetened plain soy milk

⅛ teaspoon salt

½ teaspoon pure vanilla extract

TOPPING

½ cup fresh red raspberries (for topping the frosting)

Soak the dates in the ¾ cup boiling hot water for 10 minutes, then drain and allow to fully cool. (This will soften them so that they don't break your food processor, so don't skip this step!)

MAKE THE RASPBERRY SAUCE: Meanwhile, in a small saucepan, bring the ½ cup water to a boil over high heat, then reduce the heat to low, add the mashed raspberries, and simmer until the liquid has been reduced by half, about 10 minutes. Remove from the heat and set aside to allow sauce to fully cool. Then transfer the raspberry sauce to a blender and blend until smooth. Set aside.

MAKE THE BATTER: Preheat the oven to 350°F and line a 9 x 13-inch baking pan with parchment paper (for easy cleanup). Place the soaked dates, oat flour, cocoa powder, baking soda, honey, and soy milk in a food processor and pulse until smooth. Turn off the food processor and fold in the cooled raspberry sauce with a spatula, making a swirl pattern with the sauce. Pour the batter into the prepared pan and bake for 20 minutes.

MAKE THE ICING: While the brownies are baking, mix together the icing ingredients in a food processor until well blended and refrigerate to allow the icing to set.

Remove the brownies from the oven and allow to cool completely. Remove the icing from the refrigerator and using a spatula, spread it over the cooled brownies until evenly distributed. Top the brownies with the fresh raspberries. Allow the brownies to set overnight in the fridge before serving. Cut into squares, and serve.

Guilt-Free Peanut Butter Fudge

Not only is this recipe wonderfully satisfying and delicious, but if eaten in moderation, it's very healthy for you too! It's rich tasting and filling, so a little square of fudge goes a long way. And the best part? There are only a few ingredients and it takes just minutes to make! Unlike most traditional fudge recipes, there's no cream, corn syrup, refined sugar, or butter, and it is a lot lower in fat than your standard fudge too, yet it still tastes like honest-to-goodness peanut butter fudge. So go ahead and let yourself indulge in a few squares of this thoroughly enjoyable, guilt-free treat! Yield: 77 squares

2 cups smooth, no-sugar-added, reduced-fat, unsalted peanut butter

½ cup nonfat milk powder

1 cup honey

2 teaspoons pure vanilla extract

½ cup unsweetened soy milk

Line an 11 x 17 metal baking sheet with parchment paper. Fill the bottom part of a double-boiler two-thirds full with water. Bring to a rolling boil over high heat.

Meanwhile, place all the ingredients in a food processor and pulse until fully combined. Using a heatproof spatula, transfer the contents of the food processor to the top of the double boiler, stirring constantly to break up and melt the peanut butter mixture and also to keep it from burning. Cook for 5 to 7 minutes, or until the mixture has melted into a semiliquid, with a soft, easy-to-stir consistency. Then remove from the heat and pour into the prepared brownie pan, evenly spreading the mixture across the pan until it's completely covered with fudge to about a ¾-inch thickness. Cover with plastic wrap and freeze for 1½ to 2 hours.

Remove from the freezer and cut into 24 squares with a large chef's knife. Be sure to cut into the fudge deeply, all the way through, to separate each piece from the others. Transfer the squares to an airtight container, separating each layer of fudge with a piece of parchment paper to keep the pieces from sticking together. (They should easily lift from the pan.) Refrigerate until ready to serve.

Hazelnut-Chocolate Mousse Pudding

This dish is made without any added saturated fat or refined sugar. It makes a great post-exercise recovery snack, as it's got the recommended 4:1 ratio of carbs to protein. It's also low-fat. So that way, your body gets the glycogen replenishment and muscle recovery and repair that it needs while at the same time, burning off the food you just ingested and hopefully also some body fat. This is known as the "afterburn" effect, in which the body burns calories at a higher rate immediately following exercise. This is why it's important to fuel your body with quality carbs and lean proteins within 15 minutes of finishing a workout. Yield: 1 cup, 2 to 4 servings

½ cup pitted dried Deglet Noor (common) dates

½ cup whole hazelnuts, skinned (see note)

3 tablespoons unsweetened natural cocoa powder

½ cup light silken tofu

½ cup plain, unsweetened soy milk

1 teaspoon pure vanilla extract

⅛ teaspoon salt

Soak the dates in 1 cup boiling water for 15 to 20 minutes until softened. Then drain, allow to fully cool, and squeeze to remove any excess water. Add all the ingredients to a food processor and process for about 1 full minute, until smooth. Transfer the pudding to dishes and serve.

Chef's Notes: Believe it or not, I've found whole, skinned hazelnuts at Target (in their supermarket section) of all places, but I bet you could probably also find them at a place like Whole Foods, Wegmans, or Trader Joe's. A generic supermarket might even carry them as well. Best to call ahead before visiting. And of course, you can always order them online. To turn this recipe into a Nutella-like spread, simply omit the soy milk.

Mango Tart with Cardamom & Saffron

This delicious dessert pairs the tanginess of mango and lemon with the warm flavors of cardamom and saffron for balance and contrast. Instead of resorting to the usual baker's tricks of making tarts with butter and refined sugar, this recipe relies upon the healthy omega-3 and omega-6 oils in walnuts to help bind the crust and uses honey to naturally sweeten this tart. Yield: 1 (8-inch) pie, 6 to 8 servings

CRUST

1¼ cups oats

1 cup chopped walnuts

2 tablespoons honey

1 teaspoon pure vanilla extract

1 teaspoon freshly squeezed lemon juice

¼ teaspoon salt

¼ teaspoon ground cardamom

2 tablespoons ice water

FILLING

¾ cup cold water

¼ cup arrowroot powder

4 cups peeled, sliced yellow mango, in bite-size pieces (about 3 medium yellow mangoes)

¼ cup honey

1 teaspoon grated lemon zest

1 tablespoon lemon juice

½ teaspoon pure vanilla extract

½ teaspoon ground cardamom

1 teaspoon saffron, soaked in 2 tablespoons plain soy milk

¼ teaspoon salt

MAKE THE CRUST: Place the oats in a food processor and process until they turn into a fine powder. Next, add the walnuts, honey, vanilla, lemon juice, salt, and cardamom, and process until the mixture forms a smooth paste. Pour in the ice water and process just until the mixture achieves a doughlike consistency. Do not overmix, or the crust will become too hard when baked. Remove the mixture from the food processor, scraping out remaining bits with a spatula. Using your hands, form into a dough ball, cover with plastic wrap, and freeze for 30 minutes. Make the filling while you wait.

MAKE THE FILLING: Combine the cold water and arrowroot in a small bowl to make a slurry; stir together until smooth and also to break up any clumps. Set aside. Combine the mangoes, honey, lemon zest, lemon juice, vanilla, cardamom, saffron mixture, salt, and arrowroot slurry in a large saucepan and cook over medium heat. Stir with a heatproof spatula, continuously folding over the mixture until the honey has dissolved and the slurry has adequately thickened the filling mixture. The white color of the slurry should completely disappear by the time the filling is finished cooking. Remove from the heat and allow to cool.

ASSEMBLE THE TART: Remove the dough from the freezer. If the dough is too dry, add a small amount of water to the ball before rolling it out. For easy cleanup, spread waxed paper onto a clean, flat work surface. Using a rolling pin, roll out the dough onto the waxed paper into a large circle until it's about a ¼ inch thick. Place an 8-inch pie plate facedown onto the rolled-out dough, positioning it so that it's lined up centered on the dough. Lift up the waxed paper and gingerly flip it over so that the crust is now on top of the pie plate. Be sure to hold onto both the pie plate and the waxed paper while flipping them over. (If you don't feel comfortable doing this, you can also lift up the waxed paper and flip the dough over into the pie plate.) Mold the crust to the pie plate, pressing the dough down to cover the bottom and sides of the pie plate. Perforate the sides and bottom of the crust with a fork, so it won't rise up from the pie plate as it bakes.

Preheat the oven to 350°F and bake the crust for 15 minutes, or until light golden brown. Keep checking on the crust as it cooks so it doesn't burn. Remove the crust from the oven and allow to cool for 10 minutes. Then pour in the filling and bake in the oven at 350°F for 40 minutes. Allow to cool for another 10 minutes. Slice the tart and serve hot or warm, with a scoop of vanilla ice cream on top.

Frozen "Banana Coconut Cream Pie" Custard

This recipe literally takes less than 5 minutes to make. It's especially great for using up leftover bananas. Enjoy!   Yield: 2 servings

4 bananas

1 teaspoon pure vanilla extract

1 tablespoon freshly squeezed lemon juice

1 (13.5-ounce) can unsweetened coconut milk

2 tablespoons honey

2 tablespoons shredded coconut, plus more for garnish

Cut the bananas in half, then freeze overnight, or for at least 4 hours. Remove the bananas from the freezer 15 minutes before serving to defrost slightly. Toast the coconut flakes in a toaster oven at 350°F for 2 minutes, or until light golden brown, then set aside to cool. Watch carefully, as the flakes will burn easily.

Toss all the ingredients, except for the shredded coconut, into a blender and pulse until thick and creamy but still firm (do not overblend, or the custard will become more like pudding). Use an ice cream scoop to scoop out the frozen custard into small glass dishes. Top each portion with shredded coconut. Serve immediately.

Blueberry-Lemon Pots de Crème

Blueberries have been widely touted for their antioxidants, but did you also know that they're anti-inflammatory, improve cardiovascular health, and help regulate blood sugar levels as well?   Yield: 4 servings

2 large eggs

2 tablespoons honey

2 tablespoons freshly squeezed lemon juice (or 1½ tablespoons if you like your pots de crème less tart)

1 tablespoon grated lemon zest, lightly packed (from about 1 large lemon)

⅜ cup nonfat milk

¼ cup nonfat plain Greek yogurt

⅛ teaspoon salt

½ cup fresh blueberries

Preheat the oven to 375°F. In a blender, combine the eggs, honey, lemon juice and zest, milk, yogurt, and salt, and blend on high speed until frothy and smooth, 2 to 3 minutes. Pour into 4 ramekins and evenly distribute the blueberries among the dishes. Place the ramekins in a rectangular glass baking dish. Fill the dish with water until the ramekins are submerged to the halfway mark. Bake for 30 to 35 minutes. Carefully remove the ramekins from the hot water bath. Drain the water from the dish. Serve immediately, while the pots de crème are still hot.

Apricot-Papaya Pudding Parfait

This parfait is naturally sweet and very low-fat. Plus, with all its layers, it's also fun to eat, so kids will love eating it too. It can be enjoyed either as a dessert or as a post-exercise recovery snack. As a recovery option, it's got the perfect combination of ingredients—plenty of electrolytes and antioxidants, a decent amount of quality carbs to replenish depleted glycogen stores, and protein to help repair the tiny muscle fiber tears that occur during exercise. So, regardless of how you classify this recipe, how you decide to enjoy it is up to you!   Yield: 4 to 6 servings

PUDDING

1½ cups fresh apricots, pitted (about 4½ apricots)

¼ cup dried Deglet Noor dates, pitted (8 or 9 dates)

½ cup peeled, diced, seeded papaya

¼ cup unsweetened soy milk

pinch of salt

½ teaspoon pure vanilla extract

1 teaspoon ground cinnamon, or to taste

¼ teaspoon ground allspice

⅛ teaspoon ground cardamom

TOPPINGS

4 to 6 cups pitted, diced fresh apricots (about 1 cup per serving; 14 to 16 apricots)

2 to 3 cups plain nonfat Greek yogurt or nondairy whipped topping (about ½ cup per serving)

4 to 6 tablespoons chopped walnuts (about 1 tablespoon per serving)

⅛ teaspoon ground cinnamon, for dusting (a pinch per serving)

Toss all of the pudding ingredients into a food processor and pulse until smooth. Add a layer of diced apricots to the bottom of a parfait (or martini) glass, followed by a layer of yogurt or nondairy whipped topping, and then a layer of pudding. Top the parfait with more diced apricots and then sprinkle with the walnuts and some ground cinnamon. Repeat for each parfait glass. Serve immediately.

Pear & Pecan Clafouti

After tasting this recipe, you will hardly believe that it doesn't contain an ounce of refined sugar! And yet, it's a sweet, delectable treat for the senses. The freshly baked pears and red raspberries create a sweet but slightly tart flavor and wonderful texture, and the cardamom adds a subtle note to the overall effect. Serve with a hot cup of herbal tea or a cold glass of milk.   Yield: 8 servings

3 large eggs, at room temperature

½ cup low-fat Greek yogurt

½ cup skim milk

⅓ cup all-natural (no-sugar-added) pear nectar

1 teaspoon grated lemon zest

1 teaspoon lemon juice

⅓ cup sugar-free pear preserves (if unavailable, use apple or apricot)

⅓ cup honey

2 teaspoons pure vanilla extract

1 tablespoon arrowroot powder

¼ teaspoon salt

1 teaspoon ground cardamom

6 dried pear slices, diced

½ cup pecan halves

1 cup fresh pear slices

Preheat the oven to 375°F. Beat the eggs in a large bowl. Add the Greek yogurt, milk, pear nectar, lemon zest, lemon juice, preserves, honey, and vanilla, and whisk together thoroughly. Slowly whisk in the arrowroot, salt, and cardamom. Stir in the diced dried pears and pecans.

Arrange the fresh pear slices in a 9 or 10-inch glass pie dish in a single layer so that they form a decorative circular pattern. Pour the egg mixture on top, making sure the pecans and dried pear pieces are evenly distributed throughout. Allow to set for 10 minutes, then bake for 40 to 45 minutes, until light golden brown. Allow to cool slightly, and then serve immediately, as this dish tastes best while it's still warm and fresh, straight from the oven.

"Peaches & Cream" Frozen Fruit Bars

These frozen fruit bars are a sweet and creamy treat that's fun and refreshing to eat.   Yield: About 4 bars, depending on the brand of mold you use

½ cup nonfat, plain or vanilla yogurt

½ cup frozen peaches

1 teaspoon freshly squeezed lemon juice

2 teaspoons honey

Toss everything into a blender and pulse until smooth. Pour the mix into ice pop molds. In silicone ice pop molds, it takes approximately 2 hours for them to freeze all the way through.

Coconut Oatmeal Rum Raisin Cookies

Moist, chewy, and crisp around the edges, these cookies are loaded with lots of healthy, yummy ingredients. Coconut is excellent for athletes, because it provides an immediately usable but sustainable source of energy. Coconut oil contains lauric acid, a medium-chain triglyceride (MCT) that actually helps the body to rapidly burn fat. Since the body cannot readily store MCTs, it must burn them, thus resulting in an increase in fat oxidation and energy expenditure. Ingesting coconut oil in moderation can thus lead to weight loss.

Organic, unsulphured blackstrap molasses, which is what gives these cookies their distinct dark brown color and rich flavor, is actually good for you, unlike refined sugar. It contains a variety of minerals: iron, calcium, copper, magnesium, manganese, potassium, selenium, and vitamin B6.   Yield: About 3 dozen cookies

¼ cup ground golden flaxseed

¾ cup water

2 cups extra-virgin coconut oil, plus more for greasing cookie sheet

1 cup organic, unsulphured blackstrap molasses

1 tablespoon pure vanilla extract

½ cup rum

2 cups coconut flour

1 teaspoon salt

1 tablespoon baking powder

1 tablespoon baking soda

1¼ teaspoons ground nutmeg

1¼ teaspoons ground cloves

¼ cup ground cinnamon

3 cups old-fashioned rolled oats

½ cup unsweetened shredded coconut

2 cups dark seedless raisins

Preheat the oven to 375°F and line a baking sheet with parchment paper. Stir together the ground flaxseed and water in a small bowl until well combined. Allow the mixture to sit for about 10 minutes, or until it puffs up a bit and forms a gel. Set aside. (This mixture replaces eggs as the binding agent for the cookie dough.)

In a large bowl, stir together the coconut oil, molasses, vanilla, rum, and flaxseed mixture until well combined and smooth; set aside. Next, mix together the coconut flour, salt, baking powder, baking soda, nutmeg, cloves, and cinnamon, and then gradually incorporate the dry into the wet ingredients and mix well until combined. By hand, fold in the oats, coconut, and raisins until well combined.

Drop about ¼ cup of cookie dough onto the prepared baking sheet. Flatten the dough slightly using a fork. Repeat with the remaining dough. Bake at 375°F for 12 minutes, or until light golden brown. Cool completely on a wire rack. Store in an airtight container (to keep cookies soft and chewy.

Beverages

Chocolate Raspberry Recovery Drink

Raspberries are a wonderful superfood for athletes. Not only do they contain the highest amount of omega-3s of any whole fruit, but they are an excellent source of bioavailable antioxidants. There's also evidence that the phytonutrients in raspberries, particularly rheosmin and tiliroside, may play a crucial role in fighting type-2 diabetes and obesity.   Yield: 7 (8-counce) servings

1 cup frozen raspberries

⅔ cup (2 scoops) chocolate whey protein isolate powder

⅜ cup honey

2 cups unsweetened organic soy milk

3 cups ice cubes

Place all the ingredients in a blender and pulse until smooth and frothy. Serve immediately.

Iced Coconut Chai Smoothie

Chai is a traditional Indian tea typically made by boiling tea leaves with milk, sugar, and spices, and is one of my favorite beverages. This recipe has been inspired by that drink. All of the essential spices in this recipe are exactly the same as you'd find in a traditional chai, except it uses coconut milk instead of cow's milk and there's no refined sugar or tea. Coconut milk makes this drink even creamier than regular chai, and that makes it extra de-licious! To reap the maximum energizing, fat-burning benefits of coconut milk's medium-chain triglycerides, use the full-fat version.   Yield: 2 cups

1 cup coconut milk

¼ teaspoon ground cardamom

½ teaspoon ground cinnamon

⅛ teaspoon ground cloves

¼ teaspoon ground ginger

⅛ teaspoon ground allspice

⅛ teaspoon ground black pepper

2 cups ice cubes

1 tablespoon honey, or to taste

Place all the ingredients in a blender and pulse until smooth and frothy. The smoothie should have the consistency of a slushie. Serve immediately.

Muscle-Building Protein Recovery Shake

This post-workout recovery shake is meant to be taken within 15 minutes of finishing your strength-training workout. It contains the ideal mix of muscle-building elements:

Easily digestible contents (in liquid or pulverized form). By making this shake in a blender, you're breaking down solids into liquids, which means your body doesn't have to do so, and therefore more quickly absorbs the nutrients.

Lean, high-protein sources containing three out of three branched-chain amino acids (leucine, isoleucine, and valine) and omega-3 fatty acids. The first aids in protein synthesis while the latter helps reduce post-exercise inflammation.

Fast-acting, high-GI/GL carbs, which favor pure glucose sources to aid in the production of insulin, in order to move nutrients to muscles and vital organs.

Minimal fat. Minimal post-exercise fat intake is generally recommended, unless you're having trouble gaining weight.

Alkalizing (i.e., acid-buffering) ingredients to aid in muscle tissue repair and recovery, and thus, counter the effects of a high-intensity workout. Alkalizing foods help build muscle, whereas acidizing foods will actually break it down. This is why it's so important to consume highly alkalizing post workout foods.

Antioxidants, for removing toxic free-radicals that interfere with muscle-building (and can actually cause muscle damage). Eat antioxidative foods for improved muscle tissue repair.   Yield: About 24 ounces, or 3 (1-cup) servings

½ cup crushed ice	⅓ cup (about 1 scoop) whey protein isolate powder
¼ cup dried Deglet Noor (common) dates	2 cups (1 pint) milk
¼ cup dried apricots	¼ cup pineapple juice (not from concentrate)
1 large banana, quartered	1 tablespoon honey
2 cups (1 pint) raspberries	

Add all the solid ingredients to a blender first (ice, dates, dried apricots, banana, raspberries, and protein powder followed by the liquid ingredients (milk, pineapple juice, and honey), and pulse until smooth and creamy. Pour into glasses and drink up!

Lemonade with Fresh Mint & Lemon Slices

Cool and refreshing, this lemonade will not only quench your thirst but also keep you hydrated and healthy! The lemon juice, honey, and mint are a particularly powerful combination. Yield: About 8 cups

2 tablespoons coarsely chopped fresh mint leaves

1 cup freshly squeezed lemon juice

6 cups cold water

½ cup honey

1 lemon, sliced crosswise into thin (¼-inch) rounds, with ends discarded

2 cups ice cubes

Add the mint leaves to a large glass pitcher. With the side of a spoon, muddle the mint leaves by pressing them against the sides of the pitcher. Next, add the lemon juice, water, and honey, in that order. Stir well with a long spoon or stirrer. Then add the sliced lemons. Refrigerate and add ice just before serving.

VARIATIONS: Use limes instead of lemons, or use both. Or, for an even more colorful presentation, add orange slices into the mix. Lemonade is great for entertaining guests: Add seltzer water and lemon sherbet to turn this drink into a punch, or, to make it alcoholic, spike your lemonade with vodka (for vodka lemonade), or add beer to make a shandy.

POWER TIP: LEMON, HONEY, AND MINT

Lemon juice has multiple health benefits. Its antibacterial properties help fight infection in the throat and get rid of chest congestion; its high levels of potassium can help provide relief from dizziness, nausea, and fever; and its vitamin C content not only fights cancer but also boosts immunity by increasing the body's white blood cell count, antibodies, and interferon, which coats cell surfaces to ward off viruses and fight infection. Honey aids in respiratory health and helps boost immunity and energy. And then there are the myriad health properties of mint: Mint is useful for eliminating toxins from the body, alleviating respiratory issues, and freshening breath. It may also relieve headaches, not to mention it's got astringent, antiseptic, analgesic, and antimicrobial properties. Mint's high concentration of the antioxidant rosmarinic acid has been shown to markedly reduce allergy and asthma symptoms. The menthol in mint not only has cooling effects but, more importantly, has anti-viral, anti-fungal, and anti-bacterial properties, acts as a decongestant, and can soothe digestive problems by helping to relax intestinal muscles. Its perillyl alcohol content (a phytonutrient) may offer anticancer benefits. It's a good source of fiber, folate, iron, magnesium, copper, vitamins A, B2, and C, anti-inflammatory omega-3 fatty acids, and the electrolytes potassium and calcium. The latter two are of particular benefit to athletes, as the first helps reduce post-exercise inflammation while the second replenishes essential electrolytes lost through exercise.

Peanut Butter Truffle Smoothie (Recovery Drink)

Chocolate and peanut butter are the perfect pairing in this high-protein drink. Yield: 2 servings

2 tablespoons smooth, no-sugar-added peanut butter

⅔ cup (2 scoops) chocolate whey protein isolate powder

2 tablespoons honey

1 cup unsweetened soy milk

1 cup ice cubes

Place all the ingredients in a blender and pulse until smooth and frothy. Serve immediately.

Appendix

Techniques

The following tips will help you get the most out of some of the recipes in this book that might involve more advanced techniques than beginning chefs might be familiar with.

Preparing Mussels

Before tossing mussels into the pot, be sure to first scrub and rinse them to remove any debris or barnacles and also to debeard them. When rinsing, it's important to run the tap over the crevices of the mussels and shake them out a bit while they're under the water, to remove any mud or other debris. Also, be sure to drain the water from them when you're done. To remove any barnacles or other surface matter, simply scrape them with the back of a butter knife until they detach.

If you examine the crevice where the top and bottom shells meet, you'll see a bunch of little protruding brown threads; this is what's commonly called the "beard." It's also possible to buy mussels that have already been debearded, so you might not have to do this part. However, just in case you do, here's how to debeard them: Firmly grip the mussel in one hand while tugging on the beard with the other. (This works best if you pinch the beard between your thumb and index finger.) Slide the beard along the opening, from side to side, until it gives. Try to remove as much of the beard as possible, but if there are still a few remaining threads you can't reach, don't worry about it too much. This part of the mussel isn't exactly fantastic tasting, but it's not harmful either.

STORAGE OF LEFTOVERS: If you have leftovers, you can either refrigerate them for another dinner later in the week, or just freeze the rest for future use. That way, you've got several nights of dinner all set and ready to go. It's practical and efficient. Cooked mussels freeze well, so it's easy enough to defrost them for future dinners. In this case, you'll probably want to remove the cooked mussels from their shells before putting them into the freezer so that it's easier and quicker to defrost and serve them.

IMPORTANT: Whatever you do, don't put fresh, uncooked mussels into the freezer, because you'll most likely kill them and then they won't open when it's time to cook them.

Cooking Salmon

Salmon generally requires 4 to 6 minutes total grilling time, or 2 to 3 minutes per side, per ½ inch of thickness. If your fillets are greater than 1 inch thick, cook them for 5 minutes per side over direct heat and then remove them from the heat, placing them on a cool burner to allow them to finish cooking. Fish will continue to cook in the pan even after it's been removed from the heat source, just at a lower intensity, which is the desired goal. This allows a thicker fish to cook all the way through without overcooking.

Steaming Broccoli

Bring a pot of water, lined with a steamer basket, to a rolling boil. The water line should just reach the bottom of the steamer basket. When water has come to a boil, add the broccoli, close the lid, and steam for 10 minutes. Immediately remove from the heat and do not cook any longer; otherwise the broccoli will overcook while it rests in the pot. (Properly steamed broccoli should retain its color as well as a bit of crunch and give.) Quickly drain the broccoli into a colander and allow to cool for a few minutes. Season as desired and serve.

Handling and Cooking Raw Chicken

Always wash your hands before and after handling raw chicken, to avoid bacterial contamination. Wash any surfaces that have come into contact with raw chicken in antibacterial soap and water. Never use a porous cutting board for chicken nor return cooked chicken to a surface that contains raw poultry juices. Also, be sure to work with dry hands when handling the chicken: After dipping chicken pieces into any sauce or breading, it's a good idea to wash and dry your hands after every two or three pieces or so, to keep your hands clean and dry and to avoid unnecessary contamination of kitchen surfaces and fixtures. Also, for health and safety reasons, it's important to cook chicken until juices run clear and the flesh is no longer pink. The meat of a fully cooked chicken should pull easily from the bone.

Grilling Juicy Chicken

It's very important to grill the chicken at the proper temperature and to know when to pull it off the grill. Whatever you do, don't grill chicken on high heat, or it will be raw on the inside and dry and overcooked on the outside. The temperature of the meat will rise by a few more degrees as the chicken is resting, meaning it will continue to cook while it's on the serving tray. This is why you don't want to cook the chicken all the way through or it will be dry. Just like salmon or steak, you want to slightly undercook the chicken so that it's almost a bit too soft but not raw, pink, or too fleshy on the inside. A properly cooked chicken's juices should always run clear. This is how you want it to be when you pull it off the grill.

Hard-Boiling Eggs

Here's how to make the most tender, creamy, and delicious hard-boiled eggs you'll ever have. My grandmother taught my mother this technique, who in turn taught me, and so now I'm passing it on to you. It's super easy to do: First, bring a pot of water to a rolling boil. Then place the eggs in the pot and quickly cover the pot with a tightly fitting lid. Turn off the heat, and allow the pot to sit on the stove burner for at least 25 to 30 minutes before draining the water and peeling the eggs. (And just in case you're wondering, yes, the water is actually hot enough at this stage to cook the eggs all the way through.)

Using a Mandoline

For the best results, slice the sweet potatoes for your Baked Sweet Potato Chips (page 130) using a mandoline slicer. This will ensure that the slices will be of uniform thickness and thus will cook more evenly. Otherwise, some chips will be crispy, while others will still be undercooked or soggy. It also takes less time when you don't have to put the undercooked ones back into the oven to cook further. Most mandolines aren't terribly expensive, but it's worth the small investment to make kitchen prep a whole lot easier. They're very versatile too. Many cannot only slice different thicknesses, but can also do a variety of different cuts, like sliced, crinkle cut, waffle cut, julienne, and shredded. When using a mandoline, be sure to wear a pair of cut-and-slash resistant gloves to protect your hands.

Peeling Fresh Ginger

The easiest way to peel ginger is by scraping off the skin with the edge of a spoon. It works even better than a peeler, because it won't take as much ginger with it when you go to peel the skin.

Conversions

Common Conversions

1 gallon = 4 quarts = 8 pints = 16 cups = 128 fluid ounces = 3.8 liters
1 quart = 2 pints = 4 cups = 32 ounces = .95 liter
1 pint = 2 cups = 16 ounces = 480 ml
1 cup = 8 ounces = 240 ml
¼ cup = 4 tablespoons = 12 teaspoons = 2 ounces = 60 ml
1 tablespoon = 3 teaspoons = ½ fluid ounce = 15 ml

Temperature Conversions

FAHRENHEIT (°F)	CELSIUS (°C)
200°F	95°C
225°F	110°C
250°F	120°C
275°F	135°C
300°F	150°C
325°F	165°C
350°F	175°C
375°F	190°C
400°F	200°C
425°F	220°C
450°F	230°C
475°F	245°C

Volume Conversions

U.S.	U.S. EQUIVALENT	METRIC
1 teaspoon	½ fluid ounce	15 milliliters
1 tablespoon	2 fluid ounces	60 milliliters
1 cup	3 fluid ounces	90 milliliters
1 pint	4 fluid ounces	120 milliliters
1 quart	5 fluid ounces	150 milliliters
1 liter	6 fluid ounces	180 milliliters
1 ounce (dry)	8 fluid ounces	240 milliliters
1 pound	16 fluid ounces	480 milliliters

Weight Conversions

U.S.	METRIC
½ ounce	15 grams
1 ounce	30 grams
2 ounces	60 grams
¼ pound	115 grams
⅓ pound	150 grams
½ pound	225 grams
¾ pound	350 grams
1 pound	450 grams

Index

Turkey Florentine Mini Roulades, 58–59
Turkey recipes: appetizers, 58–59; entrées, 75, 79

Vegetable Quesadillas, 57
Vegetables, 10
Vegetarian recipes: appetizers, 50–54, 56–57, 60; beverages, 152–55; breakfast, 38–44, 46–49; desserts, 140–51; entrées, 92–113; side dishes, 114–29; snacks, 130–39
Veracruz Sauce, 68
Vitamin A, 14

Walnut & Parmesan–Crusted Chicken, 77
Walnut oil, 13

Wasabi-Avocado Sauce, 87
Wasabi Tuna Steak Salad, 70–71
Weight loss, 6–7. *See also* Body fat loss
Whey protein isolate powder, 12
Whipped Ricotta Cream with Fresh Berries, 135
Whole grains, 11, 14–15
Wild Mushroom Soup, 51
Wilted Mustard Greens, 129
Winter squash, 11

Za'atar Crackers with Sesame, Cumin, Caraway, & Nigella Seeds, 138
Zucchini "Fettuccine" Alfredo, 103

About the Authors

COREY IRWIN is a healthy gourmet chef, recipe developer, endurance athlete, and running and wellness coach living in the greater Washington DC area. She actively promotes total body fitness, balanced nutrition, and long-range, preventative health via her websites, cookingwithcorey.info and seecoreyrun.com. Corey has written recipes, meal plans, and sports nutrition content for several 7 Weeks to Fitness titles, including *The Vegan Athlete*, *7 Weeks to 10 Pounds of Muscle*, and *Paleo Fitness*.

BRETT STEWART is an endurance athlete and certified personal training residing in Phoenix, Arizona. An adrenaline junkie, Brett is an Ironman triathlete, ultramarathoner, and rabid obstacle racer. A proud father, husband, son, and brother, Brett has written numerous fitness books including *7 Weeks to a Triathlon*, *7 Weeks to Getting Ripped*, and *Ultimate Obstacle Course Training*.